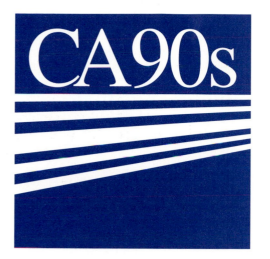

CA90s

C O M P U T I N G
A R C H I T E C T U R E
F O R   T H E   9 0 s

Second Edition

COMPUTER ASSOCIATES

There is a wealth of valuable information technology available today, and rapid advances will continue. However, if this technology does not serve as a competitive weapon for businesses, then it serves no purpose.

CONTENTS

Section III

The Enterprise Software Solutions

NOTES TO THE SECOND EDITION

The information systems industry and its clients are in the throes of a dramatic transition as new technologies, low-cost processing and extensive networks turn familiar computing environments upside down. New concepts, new trends and new technologies present challenges as great as the opportunities.

The Second Edition of CA90s: Computing Architecture For The 90s *extends the description of CA90s and the solutions it encompasses with greater emphasis on the impact that new technological and business changes have had on the information systems industry.*

While the strategy and design of CA90s remains the same, virtually every chapter of this edition has been expanded and enhanced. In particular, new material has been added to better address the emerging technologies, business requirements and computing environments of the 90s, such as downsizing, distributed processing, open system architectures and mixed environments.

PREFACE

Calvin Coolidge once said, "The business of America is business." If he were alive today he might say with equal clarity, "The business of information technology is serving business."

Profitability motivates every company. Information technology companies derive their profits by helping other businesses succeed. In light of this simple relationship, why has the information technology industry, a service industry, become such a complicated morass of jargon and mysticism that it often hinders rather than helps business? It has become so complex and convoluted that business leaders are being held hostage by their own technical experts who are, in turn, held hostage by computer hardware and software companies.

These technology companies are to blame for the current out-of-control state of information technology. As part of an industry just emerging from its infancy, these companies have continually defined and redefined market needs and technology standards in order to sell more product. User businesses, naturally seeking any help that promised to improve the bottom line, have been cajoled into continuously snapping up the "latest and greatest" technology without really knowing whether the previous "latest and greatest" provided any monetary reward. Often these new technologies did not even complement the technology businesses had already acquired, resulting in today's confusing conglomeration of hardware and software. This unproductive process will continue as long as business leaders permit it.

There is a wealth of valuable information technology available today, and rapid advances will continue. However, if this technology does not serve as a competitive weapon for businesses, then it serves no purpose.

Computer Associates believes it is time for the information systems industry to stop introducing revolutionary technologies that are simply self-serving. Rather, we must take responsibility to convert revolutionary technology to evolutionary solutions that serve the real-world needs of businesses.

The intention of this book is to inform you about how Computer Associates intends to place information technology at your service, giving control back to you. We realize that other information technology companies are promising sanctuary. But, consider their motivations. Are they merely offering elegant solutions in search of problems?

There is no question that software is the key to resolving information systems dilemmas. The question becomes whose software to implement. There is currently no independent software company that has the breadth of technology or development expertise of Computer Associates. We have over 2000 software developers and have been developing, acquiring and integrating software technology for 15 years—technology that is not biased by the need to sell hardware. But most importantly, no other company in the industry shares Computer Associates commitment to unify and demystify new technology, so that it complements and adds value to existing technology and ultimately promotes the effective use of information systems by the business community.

Consider the information contained in the following pages. It describes a practical software development strategy and outlines a software architecture designed to enable you to harness the information technology you have today and embrace emerging technologies. Computer Associates is committed to helping you attain your true technological objective, the success of your business.

ACKNOWLEDGMENTS

The development of CA90s: Computing Architecture For The 90s was an evolutionary process that owes much of its success to the insight, analysis, expertise and experience of a great number of individuals.

Computer Associates clients were prime contributors to CA90s. Their continuous input, defining the challenges they face and identifying the computing solutions they require, gave us invaluable guidance. In addition to thanking all our clients, there are several individuals who merit specific mention based on the significant part they played in keeping us on the right track. Many thanks to Gary Buckner, Thomas Carini, Glinda Cummings, George Emmanuel, George Latimer, Gene Mrozinski and Wayne Sadin.

We also appreciate the wise advice and recommendations we received from many leading industry experts. Their unique perspective and professional counsel were essential to understanding and analyzing enterprise computing requirements. While all were extremely helpful, we would like to extend our special thanks to: Shaku Atre, Michael Braude, Paul Hessinger, George Kurtz, Dale Kutnick, Vaughan Merlyn, George Schussel, Jeff Tash and David Tory.

In addition, we would like to recognize the tremendous contribution made by employees toward the development of the technology that supports CA90s. Their hard work, dedication and commitment over the years were, and continue to be, important to the success of CA90s. Among the many valued contributors, however, there are a select few who deserve special mention because of the vital role they played in shaping the architecture. Special thanks to Russell M. Artzt, Dominique Laborde, Nancy Li, Anders Vinberg and Mary Welch.

Finally, our thanks extend to Beth Bloom as well as the talented members of Computer Associates Marketing and Creative departments who helped in writing, editing, designing and producing this book.

CA90s: Computing Architecture For The 90s is a unique strategy and superior architecture designed to meet the information systems challenges of the 90s. These challenges emanate from the rapid pace of technological and economic changes that have shaped today's business environment and will, likewise, define the successful business of the 90s.

SECTION I

An Overview Of CA90s

1. The Business Of Information Technology

2. CA90s: Computing Architecture For The 90s

CHAPTER

The Business Of Information Technology

Today's Information Challenges

In a world where business means fierce competition, continued success depends on the timely possession and tactical use of information. Over the last four decades, there has been tremendous growth in the reliance on information systems (IS) by businesses, governments, non-profit organizations, scientific research facilities, academic communities, etc. (collectively referred to here as enterprises).

During the same time, the information technology industry has witnessed extraordinary advancements in both hardware and software. These new technological developments not only create great opportunities for improved service at reduced cost, but also pose challenges as great as the opportunities. Today, information systems executives must achieve technology integration in order to leverage their existing investments while assimilating new developments. In addition, they must adjust to the evolution of new, multiplatform computing environments that enable the exploitation of these new technologies.

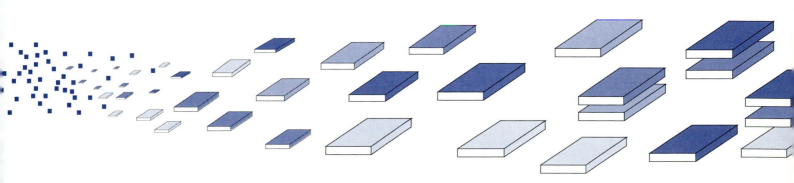

Enterprises today are burdened by a mix of nonintegrated and disparate technologies.

Information systems executives must also adjust to changes affecting the business as a whole. More than ever, enterprises are adopting a global view of their marketplace, requiring information systems that support worldwide business needs. Yet, there is a strong trend toward the decentralization of business and the information systems that support it. Classical centralized business processing on mainframes is moving out to smaller systems leading to a growth in mixed computing environments. Decentralized business and information processing, however, does not obviate the need for centralized management and control.

In today's cost-conscious economy, IS executives are also faced with increasing pressure to justify information system expenditures. Unlike the prevalent business environment of the past, IS managers today cannot request major expenditures for new hardware and software without showing a quantifiable return on investment and demonstrating how it will add value to monies already spent.

Integrate Existing And Emerging Technology

Historically, software products have been acquired on a one-off basis, not as the result of a strategic business plan. Rote functions were automated when technologically feasible in order to free human resources to accomplish more complicated tasks. For example, financial managers would automate the general ledger or accounts receivable functions. Data center managers may have looked to improve operations by automating such areas as tape management, scheduling or reporting.

Software purchasing decisions were based strictly on the ability of a product to solve a singular need, with little regard for the product's ability to communicate with other aspects of the enterprise's information systems. Software products were also traditionally designed and selected for specific hardware platforms. This meant that enterprises were either locked into specific vendors or ended up with separate systems that could not communicate.

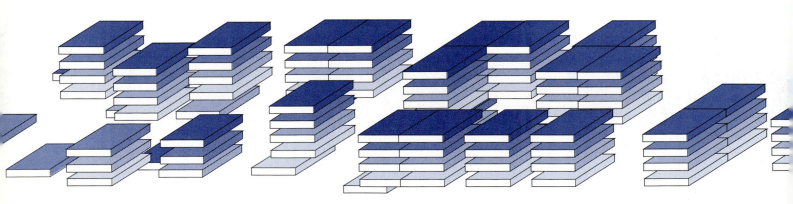

In addition, the relatively brief history of the information technology industry has presented a rapid succession of technological advances in hardware and software, offering numerous "breakthrough" technologies. These new technologies were presented by the industry as panaceas, replacements for existing, proven technology. In reality, new technologies do not and should not abolish what came before. After all, did VCRs quash the multi-billion dollar movie industry? Have airbags eliminated safety belts?

Enterprises have found that combining new and existing technologies is essential to derive the greatest reward from information systems. For example, in the 1970s, fourth-generation languages (4GLs) were marketed as replacements for COBOL. Yet there are more lines of COBOL code being written today than there were in the 70s. 4GLs are important additional tools, but they are not the promised panacea. Similarly, relational technology has been presented as a replacement for traditional navigational database access methods, such as hierarchical, network and inverted list. But while relational technology is valuable, high-volume transaction processing continues to be best handled by navigational data access techniques.

Ultimately, enterprises and their representative IS professionals cannot afford to abandon existing technology—technology that not only remains useful, but typically represents millions of dollars invested. They must implement new technological developments as improvements to the solutions they already possess.

Whether as a result of purchasing decisions or technological developments, enterprises are currently struggling with a mix of independent, nonintegrated "islands of technology" and have no effective means of coordinating or integrating them. These "islands" are in large part responsible for the inability to really apply information systems to business goals.

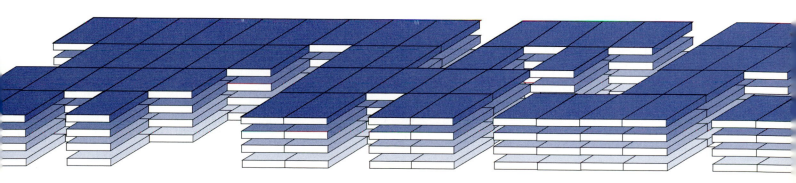

IS executives must recognize the need to integrate "islands of technology" in order for information systems to reach their full potential as strategic business tools.

Multiple, disparate technologies create redundancies and inaccuracies. Overlapping and incompatible systems often present too many "versions of the truth," varying results from the same request for information from two sources. For example, financial data that is downloaded to a PC and manipulated in a spreadsheet quickly becomes inconsistent with the data available from the financial system on the mainframe. This situation makes it hard for IS professionals to guarantee that the integrity of enterprise information is not suspect.

Training personnel to utilize, maintain and support the multitude of diverse applications is another IS management burden. The existence of so many different systems and technologies tied to various hardware platforms presents too many interfaces between the user and the machine.

Information executives have to resolve the uncoordinated, incompatible state of information technology if they are to survive.

Migrate To And Manage Multiple Computing Platforms

Adding to the complexity of information systems today are the new computer configurations that are entering the mainstream of business computing. PCs, LANs (Local Area Networks), WANs (Wide Area Networks), workstations, VAX and UNIX systems—technologies once used primarily for personal and scientific engineering work—are increasingly being used for mission-critical applications in general purpose information processing, including traditional business transaction processing. Application processing that was previously the realm of the IBM mainframe is being increasingly placed on more complex configurations based on distributed processing and high-performance, low-cost microprocessor-based systems.

While the move toward these new configurations increases the challenges of integrating technologies, there are sound business reasons fueling the move. Downsizing, the process of moving work traditionally performed on mainframes to smaller systems,

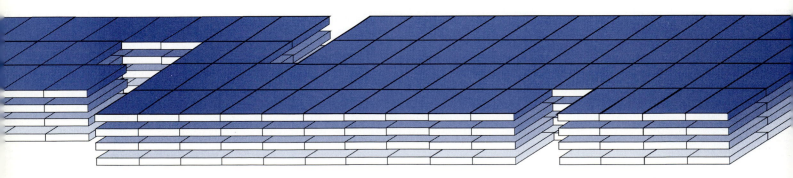

leads to reduced costs. Savings are achieved directly through the lower cost of smaller systems based on mass-produced processors and components and indirectly through operational savings with the simpler operating environments. Using smaller systems also allows for incremental growth, helping to ensure that you pay for only the amount of processing power required at any moment.

Downsizing allows the IS user to choose from a wide range of systems from the smallest PC to a network of systems to the largest mainframe, according to the processing tasks required. The term "rightsizing" may be more appropriate since it implies having the flexibility to make the best financial and operational decision regarding the processing system.

Rightsizing also makes the trend toward decentralization and distributed processing practical and feasible. Classical centralized business processing on mainframes can be moved out to smaller systems. Distributed processing configurations, including LANs, WANs, cooperative processing, client-server architectures and distributed databases are enabling enterprises to move information processing closer to the end user and the physical location where it is needed. In addition, it allows the information to be processed on the size and kind of system most suited to the task.

While these new technologies offer significant savings both in operational flexibility and cost savings, enterprises must also protect the substantial investments already made in existing solutions. To achieve this investment protection, IS executives must address the problem of how to migrate existing solutions to new environments, a process that requires compatible databases, languages and applications across multiple platforms.

Migrating to new environments must enable the full exploitation of the new technologies that become available. Graphical user interfaces (GUIs), for example, can be extended to existing applications to provide the same ease of use found in systems designed for the new environments.

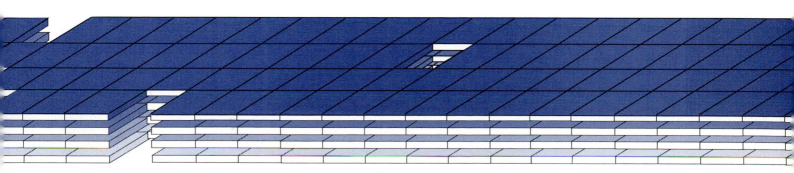

IS executives require the ability to migrate existing solutions to new computing configurations and to effectively manage the resulting multiple computing platform environments.

Once the challenge of migrating to new environments is met, information systems professionals still face the problem of effectively managing the resulting mixed environments. Enterprise-wide systems management must encompass computing on all platforms, regardless of size.

Many people mistakenly believe that the new smaller systems do not need comprehensive systems management the way mainframes do. However, while each individual system may be small, the aggregate resources of an entire network are undeniably large and may even be as large as those of a mainframe system. In addition, as mission-critical applications are moved to the smaller systems, the information held in them is no longer personal data, but rather information crucial to the enterprise.

Distributed processing itself raises management problems due to the large number of systems involved and the difficulty of physical access. Access control is a good example. Assume that security administration requires that the access privileges of an employee who has left be removed on all systems. How are these determined? How do we access all the hundreds of thousands of systems accessible through the network?

Further complications are created by the "tower of Babel" effect associated with distributed processing: with a mix of systems comes different administrative tools with different capabilities, different user interfaces and different terminology. Consider resource management. An enterprise wants to state a consistent business policy, for example, that payroll files be kept online for 60 days and then archived for 10 years. Ensuring that this policy is maintained across a mix of systems is a major challenge, especially when some of the systems may not have archival systems and need to rely on remote systems for this function.

The consequences of inadequate enterprise-wide systems management are inefficient use of resources, high costs, poor integrity and weak security. Only through centralized administration of the decentralized system can consistent business policies and consistent technological solutions be provided across all systems.

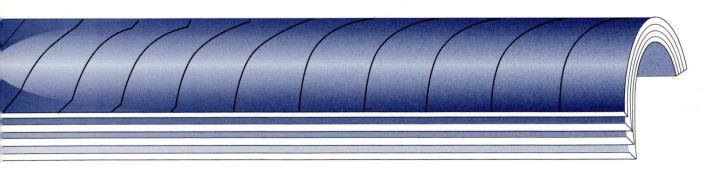

Justify Costs

In today's highly competitive business climate, corporate management has turned its eye on the "glass house" and wants answers to some tough questions. They want to know how information systems executives are going to gain control of the systems they already have today before investing heavily in additional capacity and new capabilities. They are asking, "What have we gotten for the money we have spent so far? How can we leverage the investments we've already made? How will new systems fit in with our existing ones?"

In order to satisfy corporate management, information systems executives will need to spend smarter to bring order to the often chaotic state of enterprise-wide computing. They will need to embrace the new trends and new technologies that promise significant cost savings. For example, substantial financial benefits can be achieved through rightsizing, as computing tasks can be matched to the size processor that offers the best price/performance ratio.

Major cost reductions can also be achieved by migrating to the "open system" architectures that provide vendor independence. The term "open systems" refers to the use of computers based on industry standard hardware and software components, such as the UNIX and PC-DOS/MS-DOS operating system. Adoption of open systems gives the IS user operational flexibility as well as the upper hand over the system vendor, encouraging competition and forcing the vendor to reduce costs.

Information systems executives will be able to justify expenditures only if the new, cost-efficient systems they anticipate acquiring do not render existing systems obsolete. The ability to leverage investments already made in existing systems is the key to achieving the promised cost savings of the new technologies.

Even if this is not the time for every IS professional to dramatically alter the way their information processing is performed, every investment decision today must be made with consideration for its bottom-line consequences in the changing world of tomorrow.

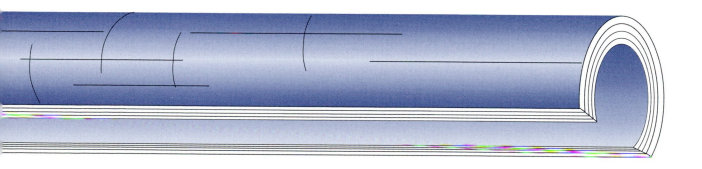

IS executives must leverage existing investments in hardware, software and expertise while capitalizing on the cost savings available from new trends and technologies such as "open system" architectures and "rightsizing."

Overcoming Information Challenges With CA90s

CA90s: Computing Architecture For The 90s is a software architecture, or blueprint, designed to give information systems control back to the enterprise. Computer Associates engineered CA90s to integrate the proliferation of technologies and standards available today, to ease migration to new technologies and to enable the effective automation and management of the new multiple platform environments that result.

Computer Associates has followed a consistent strategy, one that combines internal development, technology acquisition and extensive product integration. This strategy has enabled CA to assemble a wealth of technology and expertise embodied in the wide range of software solutions it offers across operating systems and hardware platforms. CA90s is a blueprint for the continuing development of all CA software.

It's No Mystery

Software is the key to overcoming the challenges facing IS professionals today and in the future. Hardware is becoming a commodity, merely providing the raw processing power required to drive information systems. Software already drives the purchase of desktop systems where hardware selection is simply a matter of which configuration best meets the requirements of the software.

Even hardware companies have recognized the increasing importance of software. Several hardware vendors have based their corporate strategies on software, proposing their own software architectures. Like CA90s, these architectures will be valuable in the effort to gain control of information systems. They underscore the "coming of age" of software and begin the process of establishing the "manufacturing" standards that exist in more mature industries.

Hardware sales, of course, are still the ultimate goal of hardware vendors. Their software architectures focus on a subset of their proprietary platforms, which represent only a portion of the information technology that must be reconciled at most enterprises today. Furthermore, the hardware vendor architectures often require that

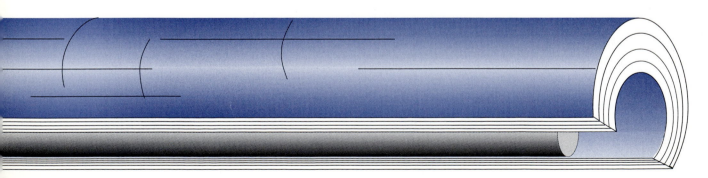

enterprises forsake their current investments in software to invest in applications that comply with new architectural standards. These architectures will clearly help hardware sales, but they will not, necessarily, resolve today's real-world technology needs.

CA90s Is Different

CA90s is unlike any other software architecture. It is without hardware bias. Nor does it add to the abundance of proprietary standards that exist today. Instead, CA90s unifies these disparate standards to achieve the synergy required of information systems.

In addition, CA90s as an architecture is complete. The technology supporting it will be extended and improved, but the blueprint is set. While other architectures require users to patiently await the creation of software to conform to new standards, CA90s is founded on the technology residing in over 200 existing CA software solutions. These solutions support over 30 computer operating systems from dozens of hardware vendors, and encompass almost every area of business software.

CA90s is a software architecture that addresses the immediate need to bring order to information systems. This comprehensive architecture integrates the various "islands of technology" that perform essential business functions in all enterprises. CA90s provides the compatible environment across operating systems and hardware platforms that is essential to implementing new technologies while preserving investments in existing solutions. The real-world business solutions of CA90s enable the cost-effective management of existing computing environments, as well as the complex multiple platform environments that exist today and will become more prevalent in the future.

Computer Associates has worked closely with its clients throughout its history, always adjusting its development strategy to address their real-world business priorities. This practical approach has led methodically to CA90s, a software architecture that will move information technology back to the asset column of the enterprise balance sheet.

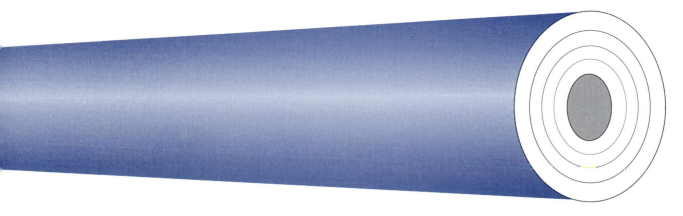

CA90s meets the information challenges by unifying the various "islands of technology" and disparate standards within information systems today while enabling the migration to and cost-effective management of multiple platform environments.

CA90s

CHAPTER 2

CA90s: Computing Architecture For The 90s

The Architecture

Computer Associates recognized that in order to address the challenges that businesses face in utilizing information systems effectively, dramatic changes were needed in the way software was engineered. The traditional method—where individual software products were closely tied to specific operating systems and hardware platforms—severely limited the ability to produce software that could address the sophisticated needs of businesses.

CA90s represents the culmination of the software direction Computer Associates has been methodically following over the years to eliminate these limitations and to unlock the full potential software holds for achieving the technological objectives of businesses.

The software development direction defined in CA90s is one that could easily be adopted by clients as well so that their own internally developed applications attain the same profound benefits that CA software derives from CA90s.

CA90s enables Computer Associates to systematically bring its broad range of solutions, covering all categories of software, to all appropriate computing platforms in a way that achieves unprecedented levels of automation, integration and portability. This is accomplished by employing a layered design that insulates software solutions from the complexities of a wealth of invaluable, shared services, as well as from the technical requirements of a wide range of operating systems and hardware platforms.

A closer look at these layers clarifies the advantages of the architecture.

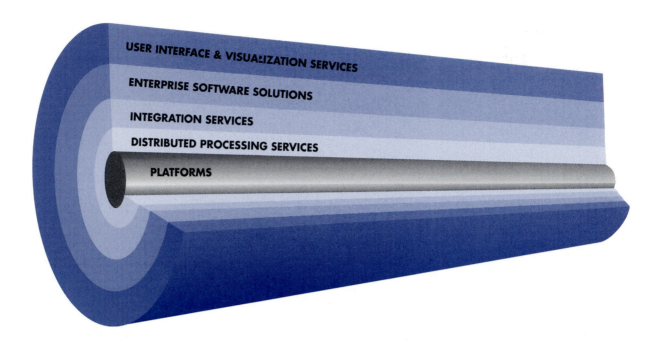

USER INTERFACE & VISUALIZATION SERVICES

ENTERPRISE SOFTWARE SOLUTIONS

INTEGRATION SERVICES

DISTRIBUTED PROCESSING SERVICES

PLATFORMS

The Graphical Representation Of CA90s

The unique design of CA90s is best represented as a three-dimensional cylinder, rather than the traditional, two-dimensional "building blocks" of older software designs. A cross-section of the cylinder reveals the layers of the architecture. This representation illustrates the dynamic sharing of services among the breadth of CA solutions and across the wide array of platforms, without the need for traditional interfaces. The cylinder also enables CA to clearly represent the expandability of the architecture. Additional functionality can be easily added to the Enterprise Software Solutions layer, immediately becoming an integral part of the architecture. New technology can be quickly incorporated into the various Service Layers, providing benefits to all Enterprise Software Solutions at the same time. Changes to the existing operating system and hardware platforms, or the addition of new ones as needed, can be readily made available to every Enterprise Software Solution and every service. The layered architectural design, as represented by the cylinder, imparts simplicity to typically complex information systems environments.

Platforms

As an independent software vendor, CA has no allegiance to any specific operating system or hardware platform. CA90s can therefore better meet the needs of clients by accounting for the diversity of operating systems and hardware platforms that actually define real environments. CA90s is able to include any operating system or hardware platform for which clients need integrated enterprise solutions.

For many years, CA has been providing enterprise solutions and services on mainframe, midrange and desktop platforms, and has demonstrated the expertise required to fulfill the multi-platform objectives of CA90s.

CA90s promotes distributed processing and portability of Enterprise Software Solutions across mainframe, midrange and desktop platforms.

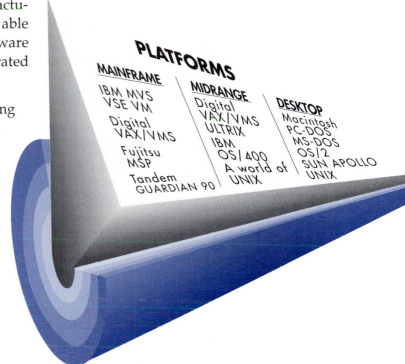

PLATFORMS

MAINFRAME
IBM MVS
VSE VM
Digital
VAX/VMS
Fujitsu
MSP
Tandem
GUARDIAN 90

MIDRANGE
Digital
VAX/VMS
ULTRIX
IBM
OS/400
A world of
UNIX

DESKTOP
Macintosh
PC-DOS
MS-DOS
OS/2
SUN APOLLO
UNIX

CA90s, The Open Systems Movement And Industry Standards

The movement toward open system architectures is one of the powerful forces reshaping the information systems industry. Open architectures are based on industry standards, formal and informal. These standards typically define the interfaces between system elements: hardware components, operating systems, services such as databases, other high-level software components and even the "look and feel" of user interfaces.

Standards have had the most impact on the UNIX world, including POSIX, the X Window System and SVID, driven by organizations such as ANSI, OSI, Open Software Foundation (OSF), UNIX International and X/Open. Formal and informal standards also control the PC-DOS world to a great extent. Proprietary platforms such as Digital VAX and IBM mainframe and midrange systems are also influenced by industry standards, including SQL and communications standards.

CA recognizes the importance of industry standards and has architected CA90s to leverage and support both formal and informal standards.

Service Layers

Services are the key components of the architecture that provide shared functions to the Enterprise Software Solutions, enabling them to operate across the widest range of platforms. By centralizing key functions within the Service Layers, rather than retaining them within each software solution, CA is able to focus development efforts specifically on enhancing these services. Greater emphasis can be placed on providing not only full-function services, but more robust performance, diagnostic, management and maintenance capabilities than would be justifiable if development were planned for only a single product. In this way, CA clients are assured of stable, feature-rich functions, efficiently engineered to the requirements of their particular environments.

The focused effort to provide full-function services also results in a natural and easy way of introducing new technologies. For example, data-in-virtual technologies, such as the IBM Hiperspace and Dataspace, can be introduced once in a Service Layer, without requiring any change to overlying applications. Graphical user interfaces can be added to software solutions through enhancement of the common user interface facilities (again without application redevelopment). Technologies from CA and other vendors can be rapidly integrated through the use of these services.

CA90s services form three layers: User Interface and Visualization, Integration, and Distributed Processing. These Service Layers are described briefly below, and in more detail in Chapters 3, 4 and 5, respectively.

User Interface And Visualization Services

This service layer is the interface between human and machine. It encompasses the most modern technological developments in the areas of *user interface management*, *graphics*, *reporting* and *voice*.

The User Interface Management Services provide solutions with convenient access to graphical user interface environments such as Windows on PCs and Motif on UNIX and VAX/VMS systems. Not only CA solutions but also client applications built with CA application development systems can easily exploit new user interfacing technologies while providing a consistent look-and-feel across platforms—graphical systems

(Windows, Motif), character-based systems (native VMS, UNIX, PC-DOS) and block mode systems (IBM 370 and AS/400) alike. Providing higher level services, CA90s shields the developer from the complexities of GUI implementation while preserving concepts and easing migration from IBM mainframe environments.

The User Interface and Visualization Services layer fully supports important industry standards, including user interfacing standards such as IBM's Common User Access (CUA), Digital's Network Application Support (NAS), the various standards in use on the Apple Macintosh, UNIX platforms, and others.

The layered design of CA90s enables CA to program conformance to standards *once* within the service layer and allow each application to access it as needed. This not only enables CA to quickly and easily embrace new standards as they emerge, but it also provides clients with the flexibility to select either a common view across all platforms or, if desired, a look appropriate to the specifics of a local environment.

The User Interface and Visualization Services significantly reduce end-user training costs through easy-to-understand, consistent applications, computerized training and online assistance facilities. CA90s delivers the true user-friendliness demanded by end users and IS professionals.

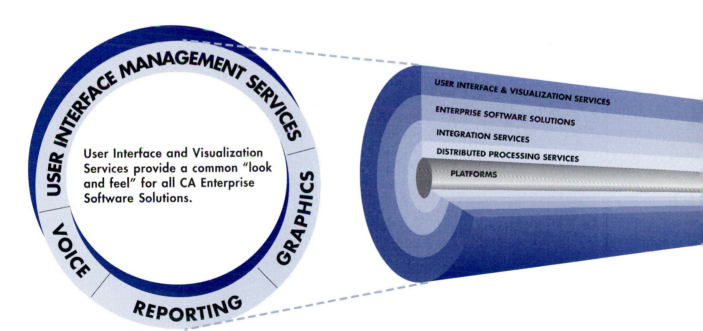

Integration Services

The Integration Services layer supports integration among solutions. The sharing of these services by the Enterprise Software Solutions raises the level of coordination among applications to a degree that was inconceivable before this sharing was developed. This greatly improves the enterprise's ability to deliver valuable information to its users.

Among the services this layer provides are such well-established CA technologies as *database management*, *security*, and *application services* such as project management, change control and expert systems. Each of these technologies is already available across a wide range of platforms, particularly the most commonly found environments such as MVS, VSE, VM, VMS, UNIX and PC-DOS. This layer also introduces the benefits of new technologies, such as *repository* and *event notification*.

The Integration Services layer supports unprecedented levels of integration among solutions, eliminating the need for multiple product-to-product interfaces.

REPOSITORY / DBMS / APPLICATION SERVICES / EVENT NOTIFICATION / SECURITY

CA Repository Services provide integration among the information needs of the enterprise solutions and the various CA90s services. The dictionary technology that forms the basis of CA Repository Services is already present in CA database management systems. The flexible structure of Repository Services supports and extends the functionality of the repository models defined by hardware vendors, such as Repository Manager/MVS from IBM, as these technologies become available.

The CA Event Notification Facility (CAIENF) is a unique technology that dramatically increases the automation, integration and portability of the enterprise solutions. It replaces the multiple operating system and product-to-product interfaces that previously provided integration, with a single, shared interface that is consistent across operating systems and platforms, enabling unprecedented communication and cooperation among solutions.

Event Notification technology not only provides a single point of communication for all solutions, it also monitors system and product events, sharing this information among solutions and enabling a higher level of automation. This leading-edge technology is already utilized in many of Computer Associates Systems Management Software solutions.

Distributed Processing Services

The Distributed Processing Services layer provides the enterprise solutions with a wealth of capabilities geared to deliver independence from network and protocol requirements. CA90s allows for the coding of these various standards and protocols, such as LU6.2 or DECnet, *once* within this layer, insulating each application from the protocol required to communicate with the target platform. Again, this eliminates the time-consuming effort and the redundancies of explicitly coding them all in each application.

The Distributed Processing Services include a *common communication interface, cooperative processing capabilities, database server facilities* and *distributed database management capabilities.*

Full support for all forms of distributed processing across desktop systems, workstations, LANs, midrange and mainframe systems ensures the highest degree of flexibility for the enterprise. Information systems management can tailor its information processing strategy to mirror the changing needs of the enterprise.

Distributed Processing Services enable Enterprise Software Solutions to implement the many forms of cooperative processing and distributed information.

Enterprise Software Solutions Layer

The Enterprise Software Solutions layer consists of applications, in many cases already market leaders in their respective categories, that address virtually all areas of automated information processing. These software solutions utilize the CA90s services to enhance integration, portability and ease of use. The benefits that accrue to the enterprise from this methodology increase geometrically as more enterprise solutions are implemented.

Enterprise Software Solutions from Computer Associates include the functional areas of *Systems Management Software, Information Management Software* and *Business Applications Software.* These areas are described in detail in Chapters 6, 7 and 8, respectively.

Systems Management Software

CA Systems Management Software leads the industry in its ability to provide true integration of functions for all critical areas of the data center. The Systems Management Software solutions enable IS organizations to meet and improve established system service levels of performance, reliability and availability, to control the overall cost of information systems and to completely secure and control access to critical information and applications. The integrated solutions effectively automate data center operations within a single system or across a heterogeneous network.

Systems Management Software includes the following functional areas: Automated Production Control; Automated Storage Management; Security, Control and Audit; Performance Management and Accounting; and Data Center Administration.

Information Management Software

CA Information Management Software is unique in its integration of relational, SQL-based technology with existing high-performance navigational database management systems. Proven industrial-strength application development systems support production-oriented, transaction processing environments as well as multi-platform, networked environments suitable for distributed processing, such as workstation and LAN configurations with both graphical and character-based user interfaces. Organizations are able to build modern applications while protecting their existing investments in data, applications and expertise.

The Information Management Software solutions address the areas of Database Management, Dictionary/Repository Support and Software Engineering, including Life Cycle Management and Application Development Systems.

Business Applications Software

CA Business Applications Software includes high-performance, function-rich solutions which make extensive use of CA90s Service Layers to provide multi-platform support, database management, distributed processing and security integration. This level of functional integration is unmatched in the industry. Business Applications address the entire business cycle, integrating specific business functions with advanced analytical capabilities.

The Business Applications Software solutions address both vertical and horizontal markets in such areas as Financial Management, Human Resource Management, Manufacturing Management and Distribution Management.

The Guiding Principles

CA90s consists of not only the structural design of a computing architecture, but also the underlying "guiding principles" of that design. These unique guiding principles have governed and will continue to govern new product development, technology acquisition and the enhancement of CA software. Adherence to these guiding principles, which are closely aligned with clients' needs, further sets CA solutions apart from other vendors' software products.

By promoting the following guiding principles, CA90s is the only software architecture that successfully addresses the critical issues facing information systems and enterprises in the 90s.

To Preserve Clients' Investments In Hardware, Software And Expertise, While Enabling Them To Take Advantage Of Emerging Technologies

Existing hardware and software technology should not have to be discarded to take advantage of new developments.

Computer Associates recognizes the vital role existing technology plays in enterprises today as well as the investments that have been made in current systems and the people who use them. One of the fundamental principles of CA90s is to preserve existing investments, while enabling clients to apply new technologies to those investments.

For example, most enterprises have vast portfolios of applications, developed over decades, residing in high-performance navigational databases. Although relational database management offers many benefits, it does not invalidate what exists. CA90s achieves the best, most cost-effective solution by integrating the two technologies, navigational and relational, within a single database management system.

To Endorse And Enhance Established Industry Architectures And Standards

Also fundamental to CA90s is the endorsement by Computer Associates of IBM's System Application Architecture (SAA), Digital Equipment Corporation's Network Application Support (NAS), as well as other established standards.

More importantly, CA90s extends the benefits of these industry architectures and standards to platforms outside their own definition. CA90s also offers a higher level of service functionality for these standards than that offered by hardware vendors. Through CA90s, for example, CA Financial Management Software provides a user interface for the PC-DOS operating system that follows the IBM SAA Common User Access (CUA) guidelines. This approach extends the benefits of SAA to a non-SAA platform. Similarly, before IBM included the VSE/ESA operating system in SAA, CA Systems Management Software was able to extend CUA guidelines for user interfacing to VSE platforms.

To Promote The Integration Of Software Solutions Across Product Families, Operating Systems And Hardware Platforms

When software applications are able to share both common functions and the benefits of concurrent enhancement, an exponentially higher degree of functional integration is achieved. This enhanced integration also improves operating efficiency by reducing redundant functions and the extraneous storage and processing requirements that accompany them. CA90s extends these benefits across the widest range of product operating systems and hardware platforms.

Each CA software application offers individual benefits to the user. By integrating solutions within and across functional families, they build on each others' strengths, offering a whole that is far greater than the sum of its parts. For example, CA Financial Management Software has become much more valuable to clients through its unique integration with CA database management services, security services, distributed processing services and common user interfacing services, as well as through its ability to run on a variety of computing platforms.

To Enhance And Extend Distributed Processing Across Multiple Operating Systems And Hardware Platforms

Most enterprises are increasing the distribution of information processing to various combinations of mainframe, midrange and desktop platforms. This enables decentralized operations and takes advantage of the increased price/performance and end user productivity that result from using the computing solution most appropriate to the task.

The layered design of CA90s facilitates disciplined distributed processing of Enterprise Software Solutions across multiple operating systems and hardware platforms. Computer Associates application development systems, for example, allow clients to create applications that interoperate between mainframe, midrange and workstation while ensuring data integrity and security.

To Facilitate The Portability Of Software Solutions, Engineered For Efficiency On Each Platform

Insulating CA enterprise solutions from operating system dependencies through the layered design of CA90s significantly simplifies the porting of applications to different platforms. CA90s thereby enables the selection of enterprise solutions strictly on the basis of business needs, eliminating hardware considerations. It also allows applications to efficiently run on the platform—mainframe, midrange, workstation or desktop system—best suited to the task.

Equally important, CA90s ensures that solutions are engineered for efficiency on each platform, taking advantage of the unique capabilities of each.

Summary

The guiding principles and layered design of CA90s enrich the wide range of CA solutions with unique and extensive capabilities. Greater levels of integration and communication enable the Enterprise Software Solutions to work together to provide dramatic improvements in productivity, reliability, performance and resource utilization.

CA90s offers additional, unprecedented benefits to clients because it is the only architectural structure designed to bring control of information systems back to the enterprise.

In addition, CA90s unifies and integrates the disparate hardware and software technologies that clients already have, to form a cohesive information system strategy that supports the business goals of the enterprise. By resolving the inconsistencies of multiple vendors' operating systems and hardware platforms, CA90s gives clients the freedom to choose new solutions without hardware constraints.

The ability to support multiple vendors' operating systems and hardware platforms also provides clients with the freedom and flexibility to change configurations as needed, even after the initial implementation is completed. CA90s recognizes that information systems, like enterprises themselves, are dynamic and must enable enterprises to respond quickly and easily to change.

As technological changes occur, clients are often prohibited from taking advantage of them due to the tremendous investments already made in existing technology. CA90s provides the only framework that allows enterprises to evolve toward new technologies without abandoning or disrupting the proven technologies already in use.

Section I provided an overview of the challenges facing the use of information systems today and how CA90s enables enterprises to successfully address them. The extensive capabilities defined by CA90s and the multitude of benefits that result from them are explained in more detail in Sections II and III.

The Service Layers of CA90s provide unparalleled efficiency in the development of software solutions. By centralizing key technologies and sharing them among Enterprise Software Solutions, Computer Associates fully exploits new technology, reacts quickly to changes in operating systems and hardware environments, and effectively cultivates technology for greater efficiency on all supported platforms. This unique strategy significantly enhances the integration and automation capabilities of all CA software.

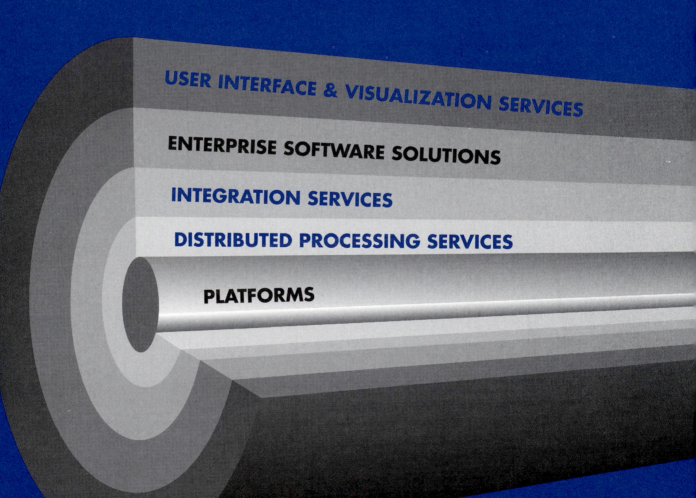

USER INTERFACE & VISUALIZATION SERVICES

ENTERPRISE SOFTWARE SOLUTIONS

INTEGRATION SERVICES

DISTRIBUTED PROCESSING SERVICES

PLATFORMS

SECTION II

The Service Layers

CHAPTER 3

*User Interface And
Visualization Services*

Computing environments have grown increasingly complex. Today, multiple operating systems (such as MVS, VSE, VM, UNIX, PC-DOS and OS/2) are a reality in every enterprise, and the majority of computing environments within enterprises also include hardware from different vendors. The complexity of computing environments can only increase as enterprise information processing needs grow and cannot be met by any computing configuration supplied by a single vendor.

One of the serious consequences of these multi-vendor, multi-hardware, multi-operating system networked environments is the abundance of incompatible interfaces or "views" presented to end users. Often these views differ with each and every product, vendor and operating system, requiring end users to undertake the Herculean task of trying to familiarize themselves with scores of different interfaces. The impossibility of this undertaking inhibits the ability of end users to adequately learn and effectively use the variety of software required to support IS operations.

Computer Associates provides a much-needed solution to this serious problem through the User Interface and Visualization Services of CA90s. These services ensure consistent and appropriate end-user views across job functions, software solutions and platforms, and provide advanced online training capabilities to significantly reduce the learning curve required to master the use of multiple products.

The User Interface and Visualization Services bring consistency and ease of use to the entire spectrum of user interfacing tools through advanced technologies for *user interface management, graphics, reporting* and *voice* services.

The User Interface and Visualization Services insulate software solutions from the specifics of the environment, so that applications need not explicitly include the presentation details, and can, instead, rely on the service layer to provide consistent, user-friendly presentations.

The User Interface and Visualization Services handle the unique environmental requirements of the many devices that can interact with the computer. These devices range from intelligent workstations to dumb terminals, laser printers to impact printers, voice input and output, and audio/video capabilities.

Architecturally, the User Interface and Visualization Services provide a series of device drivers that interact directly with each device and provide a common interface to the User Interface and Visualization technologies, which, in turn, present a consistent view to the end user. In this way, CA clients have a wide choice in the type of input/output devices they can select to utilize. Support is provided for block-mode and character-mode terminal support, graphical user interface support and output device support, including advanced function printing.

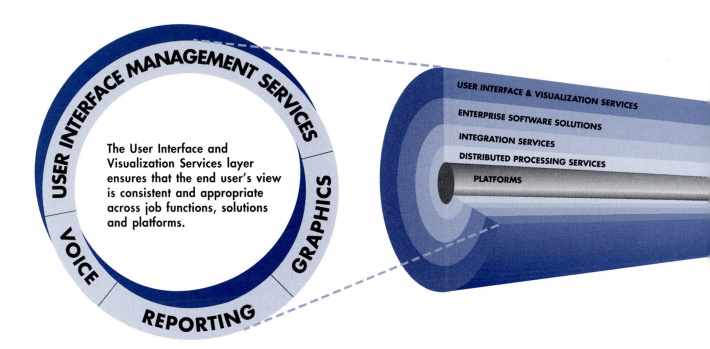

The User Interface and Visualization Services layer ensures that the end user's view is consistent and appropriate across job functions, solutions and platforms.

USER INTERFACE MANAGEMENT SERVICES

VOICE

REPORTING

GRAPHICS

USER INTERFACE & VISUALIZATION SERVICES

ENTERPRISE SOFTWARE SOLUTIONS

INTEGRATION SERVICES

DISTRIBUTED PROCESSING SERVICES

PLATFORMS

User Interface Management Services

The User Interface Management Services (CAIUIMS) enable Computer Associates to provide clients with software solutions that are both easy-to-use and consistent across operating systems and hardware platforms.

While providing access to the most modern technologies, such as the graphical user interface, the User Interface Management Services provide a foundation for giving applications a consistent "look-and-feel" across platforms. For example, when users "power up" an unfamiliar terminal or workstation, basic functions such as accessing online help are the same, regardless of the application or even the processing platform. Even when the "look" differs due to the significant technological differences between, for example, a graphical workstation and a 3270 terminal, the "feel" of the application, its logic and behavior, can be consistent.

By providing a consistent "look and feel" across a wide breadth of software solutions and computing platforms, CA90s enables CA clients to:

- Significantly reduce training time, effort and costs through applications that are easier to learn and understand
- Increase operating efficiency due to an application's ease of use and the ability to provide end users with faster access to relevant business information
- Dramatically reduce error rates due to simplified operations, reduced manual data entry requirements, and the easy accessibility of online help and assistance facilities
- Protect valuable investments in hardware, software and expertise through the implementation of consistent user interfaces and "look and feel" standards across applications and across operating systems

The Effect Of Personal Computers On User Interfacing

The personal computer revolution has raised the user interfacing expectations of end users. End users have been exposed to the innovations of the desktop world and no longer accept the burden of learning and living with the cumbersome, inflexible, unfriendly systems common in the midrange and mainframe environments of the past. The personal computer industry also prescribed how to meet these expectations—how to design systems that are easy to learn for beginners and at the same time easy to use and efficient for experienced users; how to help infrequent users over the hurdles of seldomly used functions; and, in general, how to adapt user interfacing to the nonlinear, often fragmented ways people actually work.

To enable CA Enterprise Software Solutions to meet these expectations, CAIUMS supports the powerful modern user interfacing techniques made popular in desktop systems, such as pull-down menus, pop-up choice lists, dialog boxes, etc. These techniques are not limited to desktop environments. They can make applications easier to use and more intuitive on mainframe and midrange systems as well.

The Graphical User Interface

CAIUIMS also fully supports the modern user interfacing environments of desktop systems known as graphical user interfaces, including Motif on UNIX and VMS systems, the Macintosh system, and Microsoft Windows on the PC.

GUIs provide dramatic convenience and productivity advantages to both novice and advanced users. The benefits of GUI technology are rooted in more than its attractive presentation: the fundamental operating paradigm of a GUI application emphasizes flexibility and user control, and the user interface indicates all options, functions and restrictions on-screen. It is not without reason that GUI specialists claim that a well-designed GUI application does not require any printed documentation.

As the cost of the required technology is reduced, GUI technology is likely to spread into traditional transaction processing applications, providing the same kind of benefits but adapted to a different kind of application. The benefits of GUIs are also made available to mainframe and midrange systems through the use of cooperative workstations and X-terminal technology.

The Session Manager

To facilitate the development of applications under GUI environments, and in particular to facilitate application portability across platforms, CAIUIMS includes a "session manager" which handles menu and command processing and controls the logic flow of the application. The session manager supports event-driven processing, allowing the invocation of functions in random order under the control of the user, instead of requiring the rigid hierarchical "modal" process flow of traditional applications. These techniques represent a dramatic improvement in the usability of software—and contrary to common perception, they are as beneficial for transaction processing applications in the mainframe arena as they are on graphical workstations.

The use of a common session manager, which interprets a common application structure definition and adapts it to the mechanics of each environment, allows the smooth migration of applications between radically different platforms.

Multiple Environment Support

CAIUIMS supports the wide variety of modern user interfacing techniques for character-based terminals as well as those that support GUI technology through a high-level interface. Handling user interfacing logic and functions through CAIUIMS insulates applications from the complexities of hardware environments and enables CA to take major strides in application portability. CAIUIMS effectively handles the variations between the many user interfacing architectures of various computer systems without requiring the application to be concerned with these differences. Transparent support is provided for block-mode (IBM 3270-like), character mode (non-graphical terminal interfaces such as VT100 and PC-DOS) and GUI (graphical workstation) presentations.

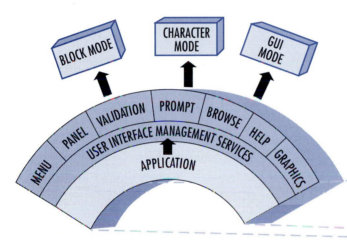

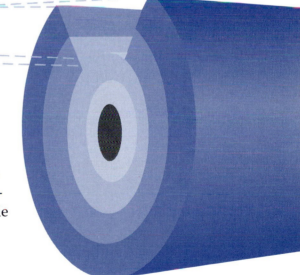

CA enterprise software implements modern user interfacing techniques through the use of CA User Interface Management Services.

The insulation of applications from the display devices allows a complete replacement of the appearance of a screen presentation without affecting the underlying application. A single application can easily support multiple presentation environments in this manner.

CAIUIMS Structure

A more detailed look at the User Interface Management Services helps clarify how they provide modern interfacing techniques and insulate applications from technical complexities. These services encompass two different categories, logically grouped by their association with *function* (User Interaction Manager capabilities) or *form* (Presentation Resource Manager facilities). While much of user interfacing concerns elements that relate to form, such as displaying information in a panel on the screen and providing user interaction with buttons, applications can also draw on powerful interactive user interfacing functions provided by CAIUIMS to improve the usability of the applications.

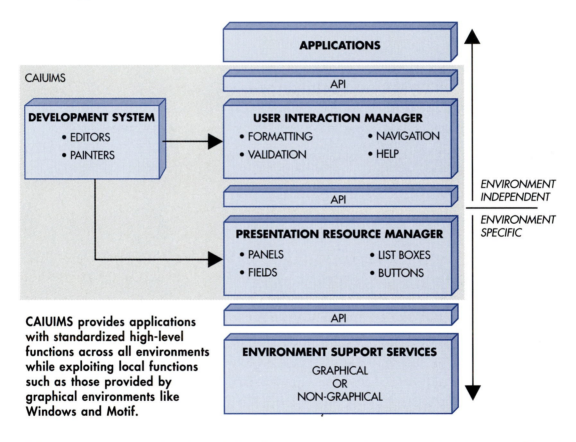

CAIUIMS provides applications with standardized high-level functions across all environments while exploiting local functions such as those provided by graphical environments like Windows and Motif.

The functions provided by CAIUIMS differ from those provided by the APIs of the underlying GUI environments, such as Windows or the industry-standard Motif and X Windows. While Windows, Motif and X Windows must provide a programmer with detail control over every aspect of the user interface, supporting any application including desktop publishing, graphics and animation, CAIUIMS is aimed at standard applications and provides higher level functions. One of the objectives of CAIUIMS is to insulate the programmer from the complicated details of programming for the native GUI environment, just like high-level languages such as CA-ADS and CA-IDEAL insulate the programmer from the complexities of pseudoconversational programming. It does this not by attempting to do the same thing Motif does, but by setting a different objective, higher level and more restrictive. In some cases, including graphics applications, CAIUIMS programming will be intermixed with programming for other tools, including native Windows, Motif or X Windows.

The User Interaction Manager

The User Interaction Manager provides a wealth of powerful user interfacing functions such as:

- Navigation capabilities through *menu* managers
- Flexible formatting of data through *panel* managers that support a wide variety of presentations for numeric, date and textual information, including foreign language conventions for dates and numbers
- Data *validation* functions including verification of data type, adherence to rules and list translation
- *Prompt* capabilities including pop-up menus and choice lists
- *Browse* facilities with automatic screen formatting, memory management and advanced search methods
- *Help* capabilities on many levels including fields, panels and error messages

In addition, the User Interaction Manager provides new "hypertext" facilities through the Online Consultant component that utilizes advanced technology to provide effective assistance and in-depth training through text, audio and video tutorials or any combination of multimedia presentations. (See the Online Consultant section of this chapter for more information on this leading-edge technology.)

All these interactive functions are provided through a high-level standardized API and are accessible to applications and CA development system tools. This enables not only CA Enterprise Software Solutions to utilize the advanced functions, but it enables CA clients to easily build applications that benefit from them as well.

The development system tools provide standardized resource editors, painters and debuggers that can be used for defining the high-level functions of the User Interaction Manager as well as the elements related to the form of the presentation (supplied by the Presentation Resource Manager).

The applications, development system tools and the User Interaction Manager are all portable across multiple environments, relying on the standardized API to the Presentation Resource Manager to provide the form of the presentation (panels, fields, scrolling fields, list boxes, menus, buttons, etc.).

Both development productivity and application portability are enhanced through the use of the User Interface Management Services because the developer and the application are only concerned with high-level concepts rather than implementation details. For example, the high-level concept of navigation among the application components and functions can be satisfied through the use of pull-down menus, full-screen menus, function keys or commands. The application does not need to explicitly define menu layout and function key interpretation.

The Presentation Resource Manager

The Presentation Resource Manager provides a standardized API for all the elements that address the *form* of user interfaces. In graphical environments, such as Microsoft Windows or OSF Motif, the Presentation Resource Manager is a "thin layer," which merely provides the standard API while the environment provides the presentation resources. In non-graphical environments, such as an IBM mainframe with a 3270 terminal or a Digital VAX with a VT100 terminal, CAIUIMS has to do more, providing the resources as well through the generation of data streams directly to the terminal. In other environments, some functions are provided by the environments themselves while others must be supplied by CAIUIMS. In contrast to the User Interaction Manager and the applications, the Presentation Resource Manager is environment-specific. Its structure and the extent of its functionality are dependent on the functions and APIs supplied directly by each environment.

The standardized API for the Presentation Resource Manager, supplied by CAIUIMS also provides useful inquiry functions, allowing the higher-level services to find out about the specific characteristics of the environment.

Application Programming Interfaces For CAIUIMS

Applications interact with CAIUIMS through standardized APIs which provide a well-defined set of functions and which insulate the applications from the User Interface Management Services.

In cases where close integration of application logic with user interfacing functions is essential, CAIUIMS can request further processing or data from the application. Control is returned temporarily to the application, with a specific action request. Once the application returns control to CAIUIMS, the processing of the entry is completed. For example, performing a credit approval on an order may be required as part of the "validation" of an order amount, and would require the involvement of the application.

To provide for this complex interaction, and to meet the flexibility requirements of modern user interfacing expectations, the protocol between the application and CAIUIMS is *message-based* and the operation *event-based*. CAIUIMS sends a message to the application indicating the event that caused a particular return: for example, a function request was made (through a menu, button, function key or command), or a field that is flagged for application-level validation was changed. In effect, navigation among application functions and overall control of processing flow is removed from the application logic and exported to the User Interface Management Services.

User Interfacing Standards

The User Interface Management Services of CA90s enable support for industry standards without requiring training of the developer on the details of the standard and its rules. With CA90s, support for these standards is coded only *once*, within the User Interface and Visualization Services layer, where it is accessible to applications. This approach is a vast improvement over the effort required to support each and every standard in every individual application, a truly impractical and impossible task.

CAIUIMS allows CA Enterprise Software Solutions to fully support and conform to IBM's SAA CUA (Common User Access), Digital's NAS standards, DECwindows, ISPF/PDF, Motif on UNIX, Windows, OS/2 Presentation Manager and other recognized industry interface conventions. The flexible high-level services of the User Interaction Manager make it possible for CA solutions to provide a common "look and feel" that is consistent across software applications, operating systems and hardware platforms as well as to conform to local platform requirements. In addition, CA90s takes full advantage of the user interfacing services native to each platform.

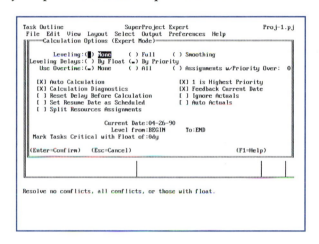

SuperProject using a character-mode screen on PC-DOS or VMS shows a menu bar, a dialog box with check boxes, and radio buttons.

An excellent example of this is SuperProject, Computer Associates project management software. SuperProject is available on PC-DOS, VMS, OS/2 and other systems. SuperProject takes advantage of the user interfacing strengths of each platform while maintaining a common look among them.

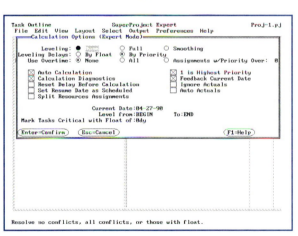

SuperProject using a PC-DOS graphics-mode screen shows similar functions with better cosmetics.

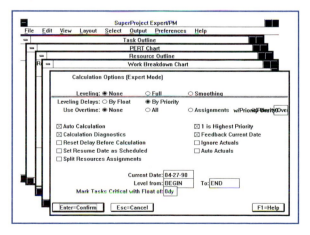

SuperProject with a GUI-mode screen using OS/2 Presentation Manager or Windows shows a fully graphical look with three-dimensional action buttons and overlapping windows.

In some environments, such as Digital VAX using a character-based terminal without a DECwindows system, there is no official standard, merely "common practice" conventions. However, there are two types of VAX user requirements that can be effectively addressed by CA90s User Interface Management Services. First, some users of VAX systems want conformance to the de facto common practices and standards that have developed in the VAX world. Second, users of an application that runs on both IBM and VAX systems may prefer to simplify the use of the application for this mixed vendor environment. In this case, they may prefer conformance to CUA on the VAX system. CA90s accommodates both of these requirements by providing a choice of modes for CA Enterprise Software Solutions that operate in mixed environments.

Additionally, support is provided through CA90s for those platforms that do not normally have a vendor-endorsed standard for a modern interface. For example, CAIUIMS extends support for SAA CUA guidelines to the PC-DOS environments, which is not an official SAA platform and to VSE, which was not originally included in SAA. In the UNIX environment, CA90s supports the industry standards Motif and Open Look.

By handling conformance to industry standards through CAIUIMS, developers are freed from the need to understand and incorporate the coding of standards in applications. In addition, changes to standards as well as the addition of new standards can be accomplished quickly and easily through CAIUIMS, where they can be accessed by developers and applications.

Online Consultant

One of the newest technological innovations of the User Interface Management Services is the Online Consultant (OLC). This special service provides multimedia tutorials (combining new video consultant capabilities with more traditional audio and text facilities) as well as context-sensitive help and advice during the use of CA online software applications on the mainframe.

The OLC greatly increases staff efficiency and productivity by providing a workstation environment that enhances the use and eases the training requirements of CA Enterprise Software Solutions. OLCs, built using the technology available in CA-ADROIT/II, Computer Associates tutorial authoring system, are available for a wide range of CA software. An example of this technology already in use can be found in Computer Associates scheduling system, CA-7. CA-ADROIT/II is also available for CA clients to use to create their own OLCs.

The Online Consultant brings all the resources the user needs to learn and perform his job into the user's workstation environment. These resources include extensive context-sensitive assistance, online documentation and immediate access to computer-based training.

The OLC workstation is PC-based with the resources efficiently stored on CD-ROM. The OLC is easily accessed from within the host application, which runs in concurrent mode with the PC workstation. The workstation environment allows the OLC to bring the speed, flexibility and power of the microcomputer to a host application, without affecting the host in any way.

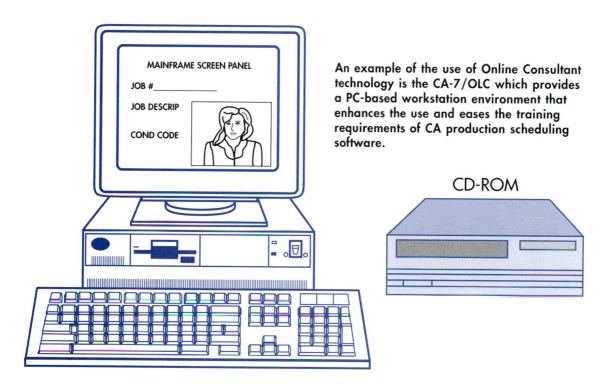

An example of the use of Online Consultant technology is the CA-7/OLC which provides a PC-based workstation environment that enhances the use and eases the training requirements of CA production scheduling software.

CD-ROM

Each OLC is designed to address the individual training requirements of each Enterprise Software Solution and its specific user community. Every OLC, however, provides these principal types of online resources:

- *Context-sensitive assistance,* in the form of text, video and audio segments, for all the panels and fields in the host application. Users can customize this assistance with a personal notepad facility that enables them to record individual information on panel and field usage.

- *The full library of user manuals,* online, complete with indexes and tables of contents. Each user can customize the documentation with personal electronic bookmarks and annotations. In addition, string searches can be performed on the bodies of single documents or on the indexes and tables of contents of the full documentation library.

- *A full Computer-Based Training (CBT) course,* on the use of the software, from basic to advanced features and functions. The CBT course can be accessed in its entirety, or in small instructional units that relate to a particular task or topic of interest. This enables users to select the precise amount of instruction they require.

The OLC provides other useful features such as the ability to use signon information to keep track of each user and his or her knowledge level. It also restricts access to personal notepads, annotations and bookmarks based on signon information. In addition, each OLC can provide site administrator access, which enables each site to provide global customization of the OLC in the form of site-specific information.

Each OLC uses CA Database Management Services to maintain the relationships among the OLC online resources and the product topics and concepts to which they relate. The user can access an "Idea Index" of topics from the mainframe application at any time, and can browse through the index, and select resources (online documents, video, audio, text segments and CBT courses) to view.

The OLC is a cost-effective alternative or adjunct to typical training methods. It is used to quickly and inexpensively train novices in the use of applications, an increasingly important and costly procedure due to the complexity of systems today and the scarcity and high turnover rates of qualified staff. The OLC provides a powerful way to shorten the learning curve and make new application end users more productive sooner.

The OLC enhances the productivity of all users by eliminating the need for them to leave the workstation environment to search for information they require. In addition, experienced users can consult the OLC for advice on less well-known, infrequently used, but highly beneficial functions of the application.

The Online Consultant also allows the expertise of experienced users, who often become de facto trainers, to be captured in the form of text, video recordings or both. By entering their knowledge into the system, their expertise is available at the touch of a "hotkey" to all who need it, and their valuable time can be spent more productively.

Graphics Services

Today, there is little argument about the power that graphical representation brings to information. Endless examples show that an effective interpretation of the information contained in reams of paper can be obtained from a few simple graphs that highlight the most important trends, saving hours of analysis.

In order to facilitate the use of powerful graphics in CA Enterprise Software Solutions, CA90s defines and incorporates standard graphics services in the User Interface and Visualization Services layer. Using a combination of comprehensive graphics functionality, common user interfaces, as well as database and communication services, CA provides clients with extensive graphics services and standalone graphics solutions that are portable across operating systems and hardware platforms.

Because CA provides high-quality graphics solutions across platforms, CA clients have the freedom to select the most cost-effective and/or most useful platform for performing graphics tasks, without concern for the compatibility of the graphics application.

CA-MAZDAMON, a component of Computer Associates performance management software, illustrates how graphics can highlight important trends and save analysis time. This graph clearly displays historical information on both network and host response time over a three-month period.

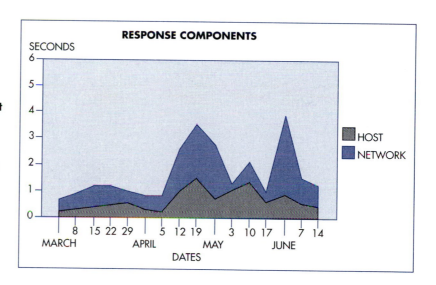

The Graphics Services components of CA90s are based on the proven, full-function CA graphics software products that have long been recognized as leaders in the industry for generating high-quality visuals. Following the guiding principles of CA90s, these standalone products will continue to be aggressively enhanced and extended to additional platforms.

CA utilizes the strong foundation of the existing Computer Associates Graphical Environment (CAGE) as a structure upon which to build and enhance graphics services and standalone solutions.

The robust set of graphics and supporting routines of CAGE are utilized to construct solutions that provide optimum graphics capabilities for each platform. For example, CAGE utilizes the graphical tools for each platform, such as QuickDraw on the Macintosh or GDI in Windows. However, in the absence of these tools, CAGE itself provides the graphical functions to serve the platform.

CA also provides solutions for the desktop computing environments that support graphical user interfaces (GUIs). For example, the Computer Associates Cricket products, recognized as pioneers in GUI-based graphics on the Macintosh and PCs are the basis for similar offerings on other platforms. CA provides graphics software for a variety of strategic GUIs including: Macintosh, Windows, DECwindows, Motif, Open Look and Presentation Manager.

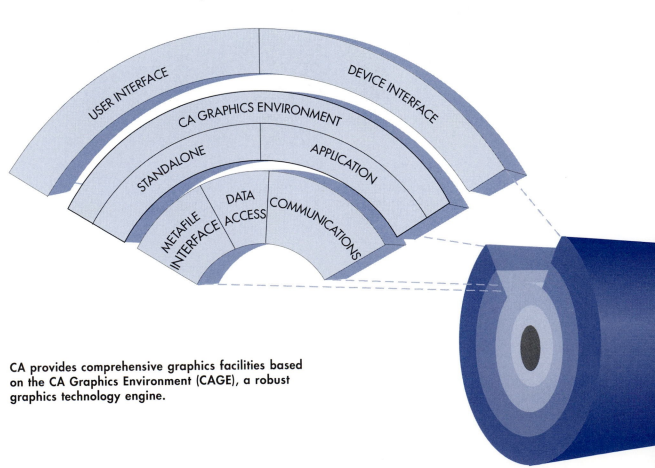

CA provides comprehensive graphics facilities based on the CA Graphics Environment (CAGE), a robust graphics technology engine.

Once graphics have been produced, self-contained device interfaces and drivers (where applicable) output the production charts. CA clients have the option of using a local laser printer or sending the charts back to a host where a powerful output device resides.

CA provides extensive high-quality graphics utilities. The CA device driver library currently supports over 300 different graphics devices.

In addition, CA continually extends clients' software and hardware investments through new and improved graphics device support. For example, CA provides a family of high-speed laser printer drivers for large-scale IBM and Xerox laser printers in both MVS and VM environments. These drivers can give laser printers the ability to output graphics at up to 15 times the normal speed.

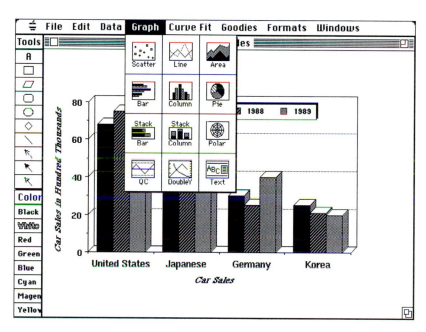

CA90s provides graphics software that takes full advantage of graphical user interfaces such as those on the Macintosh and Windows environments.

Extending Industry Standards

The Graphics Services of the User Interface and Visualization Services layer of CA90s not only provide common capabilities across all platforms, they also enable CA solutions to comply with industry graphics standards, significantly extending the functionality of these existing standards.

CA graphics solutions deliver this portability by utilizing graphics metafile translators. This functionality adheres to industry standards so that CA clients can move graphics output from platform to platform without loss of content. Some of the metafile standards supported include CGM (ISO and ANSI standard), HPGL (Hewlett-Packard graphics language), DISSPOP (CA proprietary metafile), PICT and PICT2 (Macintosh picture files), Windows metafile, DDIF (Digital object file), and GDF (IBM metafile).

In addition, CA graphics utilities eliminate the incompatibility between graphics metafile types. Through the ability to translate a number of de facto and ANSI standard graphics metafiles, communication is now possible between such diverse hardware/software solutions as graphic art, Computer-Aided Design (CAD) and business charting.

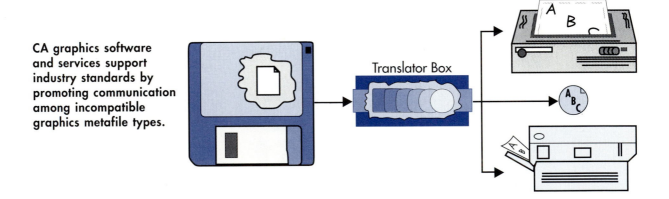

CA graphics software and services support industry standards by promoting communication among incompatible graphics metafile types.

Providing Extensive Data Access Capabilities

For data charting, the value of the chart comes from the data itself. That is why CA graphics solutions contain extensive data retrieval facilities based on CA90s communications and database services. These services connect the graphics applications to related data, allowing clients to use existing databases. Eliminating the need to reenter data for graphical representations not only saves tremendous amounts of time, but it also eliminates potential errors.

In addition, users are able to select and specify data directly from a graphics application, regardless of platform boundaries. Data can be retrieved from outside sources in a manner that is transparent to the end user. End users do not have to know the details of the data type, location or native access method, thereby simplifying the inclusion of graphics in all business applications.

For example, whether retrieving data from a Digital relative-record data set, a SuperCalc5 spreadsheet or a CA-DATACOM/DB or CA-IDMS/DB table, end users are able to use the same syntax and address the data in the same way.

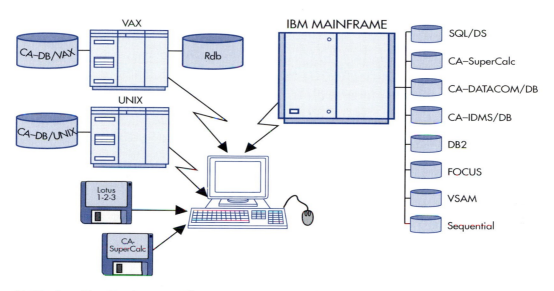

CA90s Graphics Services provide easy access to popular data sources.

Computer Associates Common Communication Interface (CAICCI) is the vehicle used by CA graphics services and solutions to transfer data between workstations and the host. Data access, including data definition and the actual reading of the database is handled by a high-level interface, based on the CA SQL Interface (CAISQI) and specialized file interfaces, that provides end users with a seamless menu-driven table selection method for identifying the data.

Reporting Services

Even the most sophisticated online interactive applications will not alleviate the need for supporting documentation. Some industry observers suggest that the trend is toward a "paperless society" which will be realized through technologies such as Electronic Funds Transfer (EFT) and Electronic Document Interchange (EDI). However, it is more realistic to expect that these technologies will coexist with the continued requirement for effective and efficient reporting services.

Enterprises rely heavily on reports and on their computing systems' ability to produce them quickly and easily, bringing together all of the required information. But changes in computing environments have placed new, challenging requirements on reporting capabilities, such as multiple platform support, modern user interfacing, relational data access and advanced function printer support.

CA90s User Interface and Visualization Services provide comprehensive Reporting Services that fully exploit the new environments and technologies while protecting clients' investments in existing systems (including the training investment). The Reporting Services provide a common solution that supports database management systems from CA and third parties across multiple platforms including IBM and similar mainframe systems, Digital VAX systems, UNIX systems, PCs under DOS and OS/2, and other environments. The structure of the Reporting Services support the complex requirements of all CA Enterprise Software Solutions.

A powerful reporting engine forms the foundation for reporting in production applications as well as in ad hoc, online use, from all kinds of data sources, across a variety of platforms.

The reporting engine is available as a service to applications written in 3GLs, 4GLs or nonprocedural application generators. These applications can do their own collecting and processing of data, using any appropriate technology, and then present it to the reporting engine. Production applications can use reports that are predefined or, when required, can utilize the services of the reporting engine to create standard reports automatically.

The common reporting engine supports sophisticated processing and flexible formatting that includes:

• Columnar reporting with control-break processing, multi-line detail lines, etc.
• Multicolumn "mailing label" type reports
• Free-form reports laid out entirely under end-user control
• Cross-tabulation reports
• Sorting, filtering, translation and grouping of data

Although database management systems provide extensive processing capabilities, it is more efficient to provide post-database sorting, translation and filtering when multiple reports are to be created from one database retrieval, each report presenting the same data from a different perspective. These processing functions are also useful for simpler data sources such as VSAM.

The reporting engine also provides extensive logic for custom processing of data according to complex programming rules that may be applied before or after sorting.

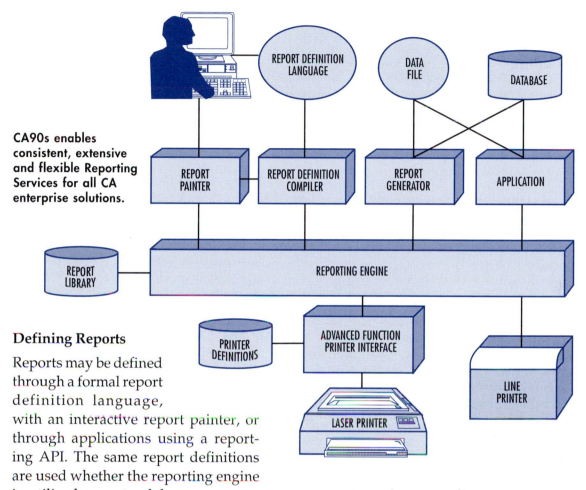

CA90s enables consistent, extensive and flexible Reporting Services for all CA enterprise solutions.

Defining Reports

Reports may be defined through a formal report definition language, with an interactive report painter, or through applications using a reporting API. The same report definitions are used whether the reporting engine is utilized as a standalone report generator, or as a service to applications.

A report definition compiler reads the report definition language (generated by a text editor like any other programming language), verifies it, and "compiles" it into an internal structure, then feeds it to the reporting engine which stores it in internal compiled form in the report definition library.

The report definition language is oriented toward programmers, providing extensive control over every aspect of the report but requiring the learning of a syntax.

The report painter provides an alternative way of defining a report, more suited to end users. Its simpler, online procedures provide access to most of the functionality of the reporting engine.

Available on interactive systems such as PCs, workstations, as well as UNIX and VAX systems, the painter provides a WYSIWYG (What-You-See-Is-What-You-Get) presentation of the report as it is being defined. Operating in character mode or in GUI mode under Windows or Motif, the report painter creates report definitions which may be executed on other systems. The report painter can thus be used as a development workstation for mainframe reporting.

A reporting API is available to high-level languages such as CA-IDEAL and CA-ADS, as well as nonprocedural systems such as CA-DB:GENERATOR, and to applications written in third-generation languages such as COBOL and C. There are no limitations on the report attributes that may be specified through the reporting API.

Selecting Data

The database and file access technologies used for data collection are part of the Integration Services layer of CA90s. The data selection facility provides direct access to the CA database management systems on each platform, including CA-DATACOM/DB and CA-IDMS/DB on mainframes, CA-DB/VAX and CA-DB/UNIX on midrange systems and CA-DATACOM/PC and CA-IDMS/PC on PC and LAN systems. The common reporting engine supports access both through SQL and through the native navigational access method of each database.

The data selection facility also supports the major third-party relational databases in each environment including IBM DB2 on MVS, IBM SQL/DS on VSE and VM, Digital Rdb on the VAX, ORACLE on VAX and UNIX systems, and various PC databases such as Microsoft SQLServer and IBM OS/2 EE Data Manager. Nonrelational databases are also supported, including IBM IMS/DLI on the mainframe.

The common reporting engine supports flat files and the main indexed file technology in each environment such as VSAM on mainframes and RMS on Digital VAX systems.

Multiple Platform Support

With applications supporting multiple platforms, it is obviously a requirement to have a common report generator across these platforms as well. The common reporting engine supports the wide range of platforms targeted by CA90s including mainframes under MVS, VSE and VM, midrange systems such as Digital VAX and various UNIX systems, and PC systems under PC-DOS and OS/2.

The reporting engine provides identical functionality and identical APIs for each platform, which allow applications using the reporting engine to be ported. Not only the application code, but also the report definitions in internal format are transportable, allowing the migration of an entire application system from one platform to another and enabling reports defined in one environment to be executed in another.

Advanced Function Printing

Printer technology has advanced dramatically in the last decade, providing near-typeset image quality at prices and speeds that are comparable to or better than traditional printer technologies. Laser printers and others capable of providing this high-image quality, as well as multiple typefaces, line drawings, graphics and image representation, are referred to as advanced function printers.

Traditional report generators provide no support for advanced function printers. They treat all devices as line printers and do not support the concept of fonts, character sizes, lines and shadings. PC systems that are regularly equipped with laser printers fully exploit the capabilities of these printers, while most multi-million dollar data processing systems do not.

Two demanding architectural enhancements are required to make a report generator support advanced function printers: an intelligent device driver and a change in processing logic. CA Reporting Services provide both.

```
REGION      OFFICE                              SALES    %  QUOTA
------      -------------        --------------------    --------

WEST        SEATTLE                              $687       87%
            LOS ANGELES                        $9,234       63%
                                 --------------------    --------
            TOTAL                              $9,921       64%

EAST        WASHINGTON DC                     $12,803       93%
            ATLANTA                            $9,113       80%
            BOSTON                            $22,840       73%
                                 --------------------    --------
            TOTAL                             $44,756       79%
```

Advanced function printing support available in CA Reporting Services makes standard reports, with no special formatting specifications, look better.

REGION	OFFICE	SALES	% QUOTA
WEST	SEATTLE LOS ANGELES	$687 $9,234	87% 63%
	TOTAL	**$9,921**	**64%**
EAST	WASHINGTON DC ATLANTA BOSTON	$12,803 $9,113 $22,840	93% 80% 73%
	TOTAL	**$44,756**	**79%**

The common reporting engine, providing support for advanced function printing, makes even standard reports with no special formatting specifications look better by using the more readable typefaces available on laser printers. It also allows users to define an advanced report layout that takes full advantage of printer capabilities such as proportionally spaced fonts, flexible typefaces, type sizes and type styles. These attractive reports can be presented on their own, or included with other material produced with word processors or desktop publishing systems.

Graphics Integration

Reports are not graphs, and complex graphical processing is beyond the scope of even advanced function printing that focuses on high-performance operation. But some graphical functions are needed for delineating and emphasizing elements of the report: horizontal and vertical lines ("rules"), areas filled in with gray or black ("shaded areas"), and graphical symbols such as logotypes used as decoration on the page. The pleasing visual effect of these graphical functions is shown below.

Integration with CA Graphics Services enables the device driver to describe the graphical capabilities of the printer to the report generation logic, and invoke the appropriate functions when required. With these basic graphical functions, many useful business graphics can be produced to improve the effectiveness of business reports.

Graphical elements, such as bar charts, can turn data in a report into easily readable business graphs, using the functions of the high-speed printer.

REGION	OFFICE	SALES	% QUOTA
WEST	SEATTLE	$687	
	LOS ANGELES	$9,234	
	TOTAL	**$9,921**	
EAST	WASHINGTON DC	$12,803	
	ATLANTA	$9,113	
	BOSTON	$22,840	
	TOTAL	**$44,756**	

Voice Services

Voice systems are a new field of technology that will increasingly be used as a standard user interface for information processing. Voice-based systems, permitting notification and interaction with key personnel through telephone and beeper networks, are already a major field of applications in the telephone services business. This technology will grow rapidly in the near future, providing enterprises with additional opportunities to apply the technology in areas such as client support, and voice notification of business and information processing related events.

Computer Associates is at the forefront of this emerging technology and incorporates Voice Services into the User Interface and Visualization Services layer of CA90s to make them readily available to Enterprise Software Solutions.

Direct user interaction with CA Voice Services, either through the telephone keypad or direct voice reply, reduces or eliminates the need for continuous attendance by costly expert personnel, while reducing response times to critical problems. Since voice response provides immediate access to information 24-hours-a-day, seven-days-a-week, enterprises can provide superior service to clients and internal personnel by making information accessible whenever it is needed.

Additionally, CA Voice Services can be utilized by existing client applications, allowing enterprises to leverage the investments made in these applications, extending their usability and accessibility through the use of the telephone.

For example, in automated production control, voice notification can be used for events such as user verification requests during the production process; notification of failures in production systems; notification of anticipated late completion of production work; and notification of operating system failures.

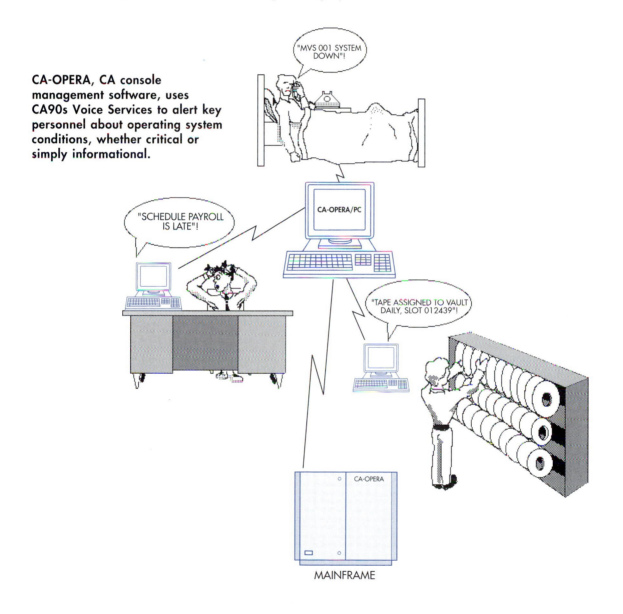

CA-OPERA, CA console management software, uses CA90s Voice Services to alert key personnel about operating system conditions, whether critical or simply informational.

In financial management and banking, voice technology can be used to inquire about the balance of accounts, transfer funds between accounts, and inquire about account rates and performance of funds.

In manufacturing, voice response can be used to inquire on the status of a customer's order or the availability of inventory for a specific product.

CA90s provides the framework, through expert systems, database management systems and attendant PC technology, for clients as well as all CA Enterprise Software Solutions to benefit from the use of voice technology and voice-related features as an effective user interfacing tool. CA-DB:EXPERT/VOICE is a good example of voice support available from CA through an interface with DECvoice from Digital Equipment Corp., a leading supplier of commercial voice solutions. DECvoice integrates three technologies, voice synthesis, voice digitization, and speaker-independent voice recognition, on a single hardware platform. All three technologies can be implemented in a single application allowing access from any type of telephone.

The Voice Services component of CA90s is also available for use in client-developed applications as part of CA application development tools. These comprehensive tools are already provided with CA-DB:EXPERT/VOICE and include:

- An easy-to-use, English, rule-based programming environment
- Automatic handling of complex telephonic processing requirements within applications
- The ability to test voice-based applications from ordinary terminals
- Easy access to CA solutions and databases

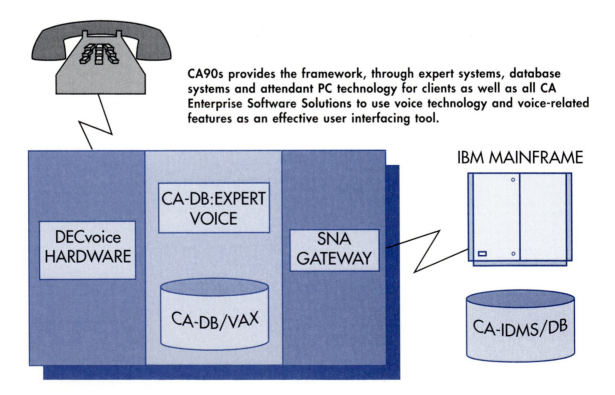

CA90s provides the framework, through expert systems, database systems and attendant PC technology for clients as well as all CA Enterprise Software Solutions to use voice technology and voice-related features as an effective user interfacing tool.

Summary

The User Interface and Visualization Services standardize the look and feel of software solutions across operating systems and hardware platforms. They combine consistent user views with modern user interfacing techniques across a broad spectrum of user interface management, graphics, reporting and voice services. These capabilities, along with the use of new technologies such as the graphical user interface and the multimedia Online Consultant, ensure that Enterprise Software Solutions are easy to learn and simple to use across all appropriate platforms.

The benefits of the User Interface and Visualization Services extend even further. Through the layered design of CA90s, applications are insulated from the technical details of the hardware devices used by end users to interface with the computer. This represents a dramatic improvement over traditional software design which required each application to contain specific code related to the hardware device. By contrast, CA90s allows applications to be independent of the presentation of data.

By handling the presentation specifications in the User Interface and Visualization Services layer, CA90s enables all applications, both new and old, to utilize new hardware devices and new user interfacing technologies. This not only extends the life of existing applications, but it also ensures that today's applications can take full advantage of the user interfacing advances of the future.

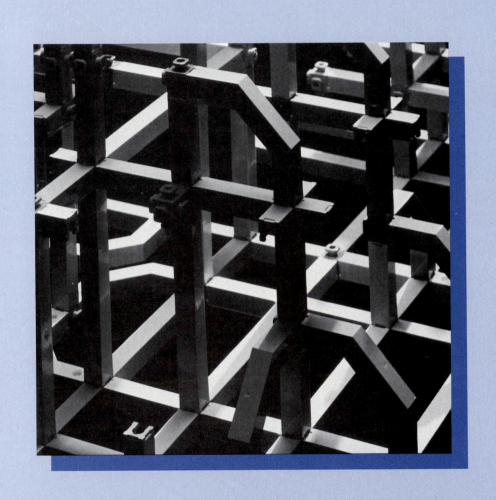

CHAPTER 4

Integration Services

To effectively meet enterprise computing needs, information systems must be fully integrated. When applications work together, performance is improved, productivity is increased, accuracy is refined and resources are more efficiently utilized. However, isolated pockets of integrated solutions fall short of providing effective information systems management. Multiple nonintegrated sources of enterprise data virtually guarantee serious inaccuracies and data integrity problems. Lack of enterprise-wide integration of information also seriously limits the ability of management to access and analyze the data needed for business decisions.

Ultimately, enterprises would like to have a single point of information management, a single point of product communication, and a single point of security and integrity control from which they could manage their enterprise-wide information systems. With this goal in mind, information systems integration must be continually improved to become more effective as a strategic business tool.

Traditional methods of providing integration among software solutions inadequately address these enterprise-wide needs, particularly in multi-vendor, multi-operating system, networked environments. Coding and maintaining the numerous product-to-product interfaces that are required to integrate the many interdependent functions involved in enterprise-wide computing is time-consuming, unwieldy, error-prone and highly impractical.

Computer Associates addresses these problems and achieves efficient, seamless integration and interoperability of applications, across functional areas and across multiple operating environments without the need for numerous, hard-coded interfaces. Through the unique layered design and advanced technologies of CA90s, Enterprise Software Solutions can access the same common services, such as database management, event notification and security, preserving data integrity while promoting data sharing and the exchange of information across product boundaries and computing platforms.

In this way, enterprise management will soon enjoy a single point of control for enterprise-wide information. In addition, the breadth of CA products, spanning Systems Management, Information Management and Business Applications, that are intrinsically integrated through CA90s, provides a wealth of automation capabilities previously impossible to achieve.

The Integration Services layer of CA90s provides:

- *Database Management Services*, which give CA solutions and other services the flexibility to store, view and manipulate information in whatever ways are most appropriate to the specific application.
- *Repository Services*, which provide enterprise-wide dictionary facilities for sharing information across all CA Enterprise Software Solutions and services.
- *Event Notification Facility (CAIENF)*, which handles the specific requirements of each operating system and provides event notification for the enterprise solutions and other CA90s services.
- *Standard Security Facility (CAISSF)*, which provides access control services for all components of CA90s.
- *Application Services*, which provide standard end-user level functions, such as decision support and expert systems, to all enterprise solutions.

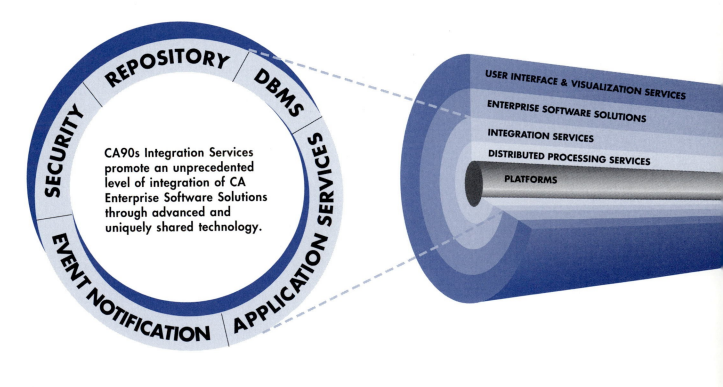

Database Management Services

Database Management Services provide the underlying technologies that give data management flexibility to Enterprise Software Solutions. The Database Management Services provide important functionality such as:

- *Data management*, easily accommodating complex data structures, and giving enterprise solutions the ability to relate elementary information in different ways. The Database Management Services also support complex data access, giving CA solutions the ability to provide multiple views of the same information through standard query and reporting services.

- *Data sharing*, allowing enterprise solutions to reference and rely on common information. This capability is extremely limited with traditional access methods. When enterprise solutions cannot share data, enterprises often end up with unreliable information representing "multiple versions of the truth." Through Database Management Services, CA solutions can be based on common information, further promoting integration among components.

- *Data integrity and security*, ensuring the accuracy and reliability of critical information. The combination of transaction management with journaling capabilities and embedded security protects the data from damage or malfeasance and from unauthorized access.

- *Data availability*, enhancing the accessibility of information to end users. Database Management Services provide extensive dynamic database maintenance capabilities to ensure 24-hour availability of information. Information can also be made more available locally through Distributed Database Services. The ad hoc query and reporting capabilities of the Database Management Services not only make critical information more accessible, but also easier to review and manipulate.

- *Performance*, providing high-speed, flexible access to production data. CA database engines are highly tuned for maximum performance regardless of the access technique used. These engines are also engineered to provide maximum efficiency on each platform by taking advantage of the performance options available for each operating system.

- *Portability*, across multiple operating systems and hardware platforms. This portability not only allows CA clients to choose the most cost-effective platforms for applications, but also takes full advantage of the functionality on each platform.

- *Distributed information*, allowing enterprise-wide applications across a mix of platforms to cooperate with full data integrity, through any combination of distributed database management or database servers available in conjunction with CA90s Distributed Processing Services.

The Database Management Services are used by many CA enterprise solutions, which derive significant benefits not only from the power of the services themselves, but from integration with other services and solutions within CA90s. Masterpiece (CA Financial Management Software), for example, shows clearly the "explosion effect" of direct and indirect benefits provided: not only is Masterpiece now two to three times faster than previous versions that were based on less sophisticated file systems, but it offers clients extensibility through integrated dictionary and application development systems and flexible end-user access to enterprise financial information through online query and reporting systems. Masterpiece, CA-CAS (Manufacturing Management Software), CA-HRS (Human Resource Management Software), CA-UNIPACK/DCA (Data Center Administration), and CA-UNIPACK/APC (Automated Production Control), are only some of the solutions that rely on Database Management Services for high performance, data sharing, data integrity and other advantages.

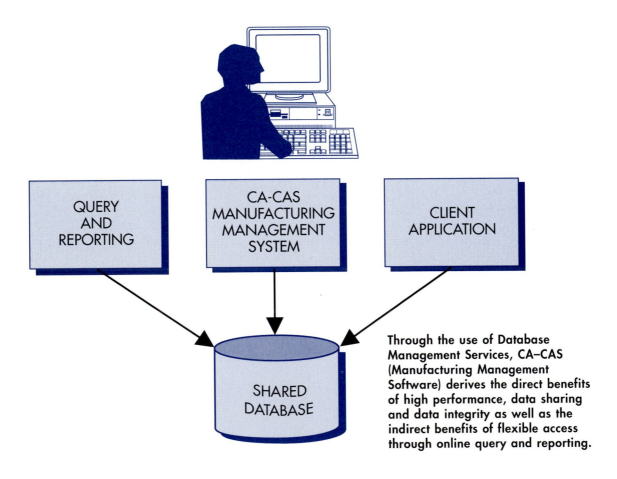

Through the use of Database Management Services, CA–CAS (Manufacturing Management Software) derives the direct benefits of high performance, data sharing and data integrity as well as the indirect benefits of flexible access through online query and reporting.

Building On Proven Technology

CA Database Management Services are far superior to other database management solutions because they have been engineered to deliver the benefits of both relational technology and high-performance navigational techniques in one database. Built on technology that has proven successful in thousands of CA client sites for over a decade, the powerful navigational technology of the Database Management Services has been significantly extended for CA90s through the implementation of SQL techniques for relational access.

With the SQL capabilities of CA Database Management Services, CA clients can immediately and directly take advantage of advanced information processing techniques provided by relational access, including the flexibility and ease of query and report management so necessary in today's business environments.

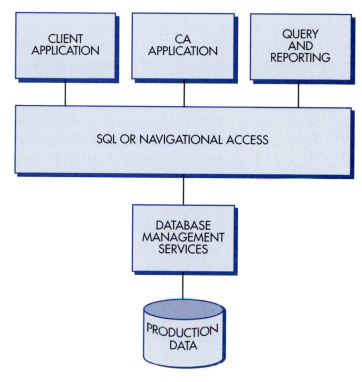

CA Database Management Services uniquely deliver the benefits of both relational technology and navigational techniques against the same production data through a single database management system.

While SQL is a useful and valid technology, it is not always the most appropriate access method for complex structure management embedded in procedural logic, or for iterative and recursive logic. For this, navigational technology is an absolute requirement. With Computer Associates Database Management Services, the complex procedural logic required for online applications that must have rapid response time is still available through navigational techniques that coexist with SQL and that may be employed *on the same data*. Thus, relational flexibility can be achieved without losing the high performance made possible by the navigational approach. This co-existence of multiple data access methods is not supported by any other architecture.

Although industry standard SQL provides a usable language for access to relational database management systems, CA has years of experience in its own advanced SQL technology, one that supports a richer set of capabilities than standard SQL. CA Extended SQL includes the industry standard SQL as a proper subset and gives CA clients the option to use only the standard SQL language, or the more powerful CA Extended SQL. CA Extended SQL also conforms with the FIPS (Federal Information Processing Standard) variant of the ANSI standard and with major industry SQL standards such as IBM SAA SQL (DB2, SQL/DS and OS/2 EE).

The Database Management Services ensure that relational processing performs well through robust optimization techniques that perform the most efficient internal conversions for all types of queries and through the integral precompiler and the Adaptive Query Manager. SQL statements may be embedded within application programs written in third-generation languages such as COBOL, C and PL/I. The precompiler component of CA Extended SQL will recognize these statements, pass them to the parser and optimizer components to transform them into an internal format and determine the best access path to process the query. Optimization of SQL statements during application development, rather than during production, saves considerable CPU cycles. Optimizing queries into access plans at compile time does not reduce an installation's flexibility, even for those whose databases require frequent modification and tuning. The CA Adaptive Query Manager component automatically reoptimizes queries whenever the environment changes.

Alternative Database Access Methods

Providing more than one form of data manipulation language such as SQL and navigational techniques within a single database management system is a unique and useful strategy that will enable CA to easily incorporate emerging technologies that promise even more powerful flexibility of access than that provided by SQL today. CA clients can benefit from the use of these new technologies without having to maintain multiple databases or rewrite existing applications.

New technologies under development or consideration for implementation as alternative database access methods include:

- *Entity-relationship models*—This is fast becoming a de facto standard for data modeling used by many advanced applications. Examples of its use include front-end CASE products and the Repository Manager/MVS from IBM. The entity-relationship model is also being supported by the proposed ANSI Information Resource Dictionary System (IRDS). The entity-relationship model is extremely appropriate for inclusion in CA Database Management Systems, particularly because it is itself a combination of navigational and relational functionalities. The dictionaries integrated with the Database Management Services are based on this technology.

- *Multimedia*—Complex and unstructured objects such as text, documents, graphics and images are increasingly used in modern applications. One of the important influences in this area is the emergence of standards for handling these kinds of information. The Database Management Services will be extended to provide support for storage and retrieval of such information. Powerful technologies that form the basis for managing multimedia objects are available within CA90s. For example, CA90s graphics technology is capable of managing, displaying and cross-translating several of these formats such as CGM, PostScript, and various document and text formats from IBM, Digital, UNIX and others.

- *Semantic and object-oriented*—These technologies are viewed by some researchers as having the potential to provide the key to significant productivity advances in the future, integrating more logical processing into the database management system itself.

High-Performance Database Engines

CA Database Management Services comprise not only the external components that allow users to access data (components such as language support and distributed processing support), but also the engines of the database system that store and retrieve the data and that provide the means for performance tuning, integrity, storage management and database navigation. Each engine is designed to take maximum advantage of a particular computing platform, ensuring maximum efficiency of database processing on all platforms.

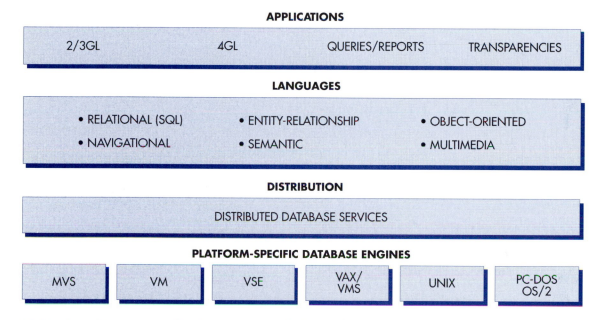

CA Database Management Services support multiple database access languages for database engines, which are tuned for efficiency on each platform. Distributed database capabilities are provided in conjunction with CA90s Distributed Processing Services.

Open Architecture

CA Database Management Services support an open architecture. The CA SQL Interface, CAISQI, provides a standardized interface to several SQL-based relational database management systems, both CA products and major third-party products. CAISQI allows an application to transparently access different database management systems, even change database management systems in mid-processing, without requiring code changes, recompilation, rebinding, or relink-editing.

CAISQI supports both dynamic and static SQL, insulating the application from the operational differences that exist between SQL products from different vendors: linkage methods, binding methods, levels of static and dynamic support, return codes, data area structure, etc. CAISQI may be used from an application written in COBOL or C as well as in CA high-level languages and systems such as CA-DB:GENERATOR.

CAISQI supports major database management systems including CA-DATACOM, CA-IDMS, CA-DB/VAX, CA-DB/UNIX, IBM DB2, Digital Rdb and Oracle.

The standard API to relational SQL-based relational database management systems is CAISQI, which interfaces transparently to CA and third-party database management systems.

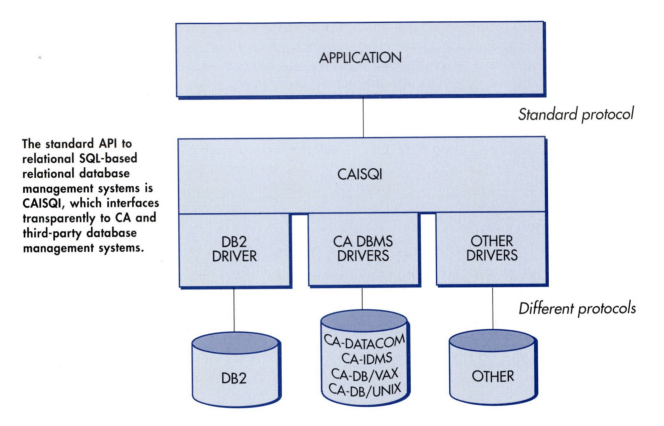

"Black Box" Configuration

CA Enterprise Software Solutions may be installed with the database in a "black box" configuration: a limited data management subsystem that does not require the investment in training and support of a full-fledged database management system.

The "black box" data management subsystem retains the operating advantages of the full database management system, such as high performance and flexibility in extending and modifying the application, while simplifying installation and operation of the application system. This is possible because the data management system is configured to handle only a specific application with known data contents and operating characteristics.

The term, "black box," does not refer to a completely closed system. A system manager who prefers to customize the database or fine-tune its performance is provided with all the flexibility of the full-fledged database, including performance monitoring and tuning utilities.

In all cases, the limited functionality subsystem may be upgraded to a full-fledged database for use in other systems with data not managed by the specific CA enterprise solution.

Extending Database Technology To New Environments

The CA90s Database Management Services provide the same functionality on all major platforms, including mainframes, Digital VAX systems, UNIX systems and PCs, both standalone and in LAN configurations. The common functionality and interfaces provide the foundation for application migration to smaller systems and for use of smaller systems as development and test environments. These services provide support for client-server configurations in both homogeneous and heterogeneous LAN environments (see Chapter 5, "Distributed Processing Services").

Database Management Services will gain even more importance to enterprises as the evolution continues toward the use of corporate repositories for which database management services are the critical underlying technologies.

Repository Services

Repository Services provide centralized management and control for all the information that encompasses the computing needs of the entire enterprise including information about CA software solutions (Systems Management, Information Management and Business Applications). CA Repository Services are based upon and extend CA dictionary technology already in extensive use at CA client sites.

Repository Services will enable enterprises to complement and be compatible with hardware vendor repositories such as IBM Repository Manager/MVS and Digital CDD/Repository. In addition, CA Repository Services will support multiple platforms and include the ability to distribute information across platforms.

Repository Technology Evolution

The emergence of database management systems facilitated and promoted the sharing of information across application systems and even across departmental lines in an organization. Each department no longer "owned" its data; the concept of information as a shared corporate resource was established.

To support this concept, data dictionaries were developed as extensions to database management systems—first, simply as a library of data definitions. Later, data dictionaries emerged as the basis for the integration of information management tools, integrity enforcement of the information definition, a centralized facility for sharing of information resources, management and control of information resources, and documentation.

CA pioneered dictionary technology with its well-established database management systems and today accounts for more than half of the dictionary market segment. CA dictionary technology already offers clients a central repository for consistent and descriptive definitions of corporate information resources. These dictionaries evolved from active sources of data definitions for the database management systems themselves, to application dictionaries for the entire application development life cycle.

The application dictionary evolution continued with the extension of dictionary capabilities to "objects," or other system components such as panels, source code, etc. Operational considerations also were included under the dictionary umbrella, as were configuration management and change control.

Users quickly recognized the benefits of maintaining a central repository for effective information management and soon needed the ability to include types of objects that were unique to their enterprise, as well as the ability to expand the type of information kept about vendor-supported objects. Users were therefore given the capability to extend the CA dictionary model with their own enterprise definitions.

Over the years, many users have added their own extensions to other passive, single product-oriented dictionaries, some of which are still in use today. They also added extensions to dictionaries of newer database management systems, resulting in dictionaries that were tightly integrated and active, but for a single database management system only. Users who have multiple database management systems have had multiple dictionaries, with no single interface or other method for integrating them.

CA Repository Services unite these multiple types of dictionary information, enabling them to be controlled under a unifying umbrella, with a common interface provided for all. Repository Services offer the reliability and convenience of a single, central management for all enterprise information.

The substantial investments in time, effort and costs that enterprises have made in individual dictionary products and in the dictionaries that support single database management systems are not lost by the implementation of CA Repository Services. The services are an extension of these existing dictionaries, not a replacement. In fact, the investment is significantly enhanced by the integration that can now exist between dictionaries and repositories.

Repository Services Structure

Repository Services encompass three main levels:

- An API known as the CA Common Repository Interface (CAICRI) that handles the interaction between the users and the Information Model

- The Information Model that describes the information structure as well as the external views utilized by the API and storage views

- Storage Management Facilities that handle the actual storing of the data

The CA Repository Services provide centralized management and control for all enterprise information.

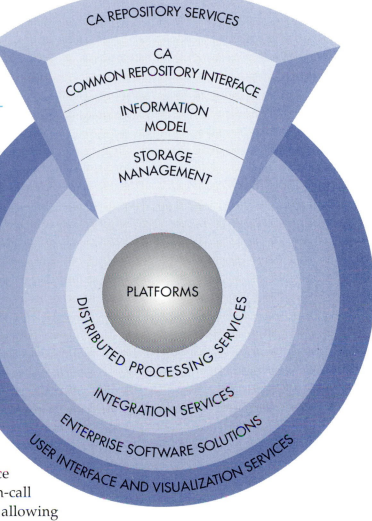

Common Repository Interface

The CA Common Repository Interface (CAICRI) is a full-function, program-call interface to CA Repository Services, allowing CA software and user programs to populate, navigate and maintain the information under the control of the repository. This interface promotes a common view of enterprise information that may be described in multiple dictionaries.

The Common Repository Interface supports the IBM SAA Common Programming Interface (CPI) extension for repository services, enabling any third-party vendor product using these services to interface with CA Repository Services. CAICRI will also support the future ANSI Information Resource Dictionary System (IRDS) services standards if these should differ from the IBM implementation.

The Information Model

All information under the control of the repository is described in the Repository Services Information Model. The model is used as an information interface providing a high-level view of the information structure controlled by the repository. The CA Repository Services Information Model follows the three-schema concept developed by the ANSI committee to solve the maintenance problems caused by applications dependent on physical storage structures. The three layers insulate the application from the model and storage management requirements, thereby providing data independence.

The Information Model comprises:

- The *external views* used as the means of communication and unit of data transfer by the API (CAICRI)
- The *repository model*, which defines the various entity types supported by the repository
- The *storage views* that describe the underlying storage management

The middle level, the Repository Model, is the conceptual schema that defines the data in-and-of-itself, regardless of usage or storage. Each application has its own view of the data (external views), mapped to the conceptual level. The conceptual level is then mapped to the physical level of the data (storage management views). If this physical level changes, only the mapping between the conceptual and physical must be changed. The application views remain unchanged. This enables changes to be made to the physical level without having a negative impact on existing applications.

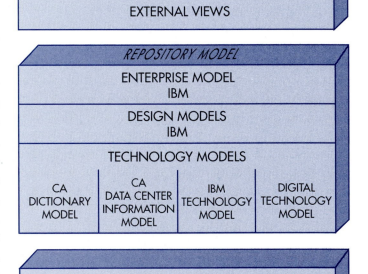

The repository information model follows the three-schema concept (ANSI) and comprises external views, the repository model and storage views.

The Repository Model is based on the entity relationship modeling technique and applies to the Enterprise Model (which defines the structure of the enterprise, its business rules, its policies, its procedures and its data), the Design Model (which defines the design of the solutions for the automation of the enterprise) and the Technology Model (which defines the implementation of the solutions in terms of the database and application definitions).

The CA Repository Model protects clients' investments in existing technology by providing support for both existing dictionaries and hardware vendor repositories. The CA Repository Model supports the CA dictionary models that are already in wide use, the IBM Repository Manager/MVS information model, the Digital CDD/Repository model, and a new CA data center information model.

Repository Services encompass not only the areas of information management and business applications that are usually included in repository discussions. It also includes systems management information, recognizing that these applications for data center activities are also valuable sources of corporate information that need to be available and accessible through the repository. No other architecture describes a data center information model as an important component of the corporate repository.

The data center information model of the CA Repository Services defines the following types of information for Computer Associates entire Enterprise Software Solutions line:

- *Rules*—Many CA solutions, such as scheduling and security software are rule- or policy-based. The user defines the set of rules that determine how the software will handle different processes and actions. These rules are currently recorded in product files or databases.

- *Product Processing Options*—Most CA solutions provide processing options to indicate how the overall software will operate under specified conditions. These options are currently supplied by means of parameters or control file entries.

- *Product Information*—As part of their processing, most CA solutions use additional files and databases to record information specific to the solution. Usually this information takes the form of logging, audit trails and recovery information. This category also includes the information necessary for event sharing through the CA Event Notification Facility (CAIENF).

Storage Management Facilities

Repository Services offer a variety of storage management techniques depending on the needs of each functional area. The four categories of storage management supported include: dictionaries, database management systems, catalogs and memory-resident information.

The Repository Services storage management facilities support a variety of storage management techniques depending on the needs of each functional area.

By supporting these forms of storage, Repository Services allow information accessible through current storage mechanisms to participate in the repository, further protecting clients' investments in existing technology. Each storage management category offers a unique level of service.

CA dictionaries provide for easy management of complex entity/relationship structures, version/status for change control and configuration management, keyword access and text/documentation management.

Dictionaries supported include the CA dictionaries, Repository Manager/MVS and CDD/Repository. Interfaces are handled by the CA Common Repository Interface (CAICRI). CA dictionaries will also be used to store the CA Repository Model.

Databases provide for the management of complex data structures, relational capabilities and SQL access. The databases supported are CA databases, IBM's relational databases and Digital's Rdb. Interfaces are handled by the CA SQL Interface (CAISQI).

Catalog and memory-resident access are often used in Systems Management solutions. By supporting these storage mechanisms, CA Systems Management Software can participate in the repository more quickly and investments in existing file structures are protected.

66

Catalogs provide for simple data structures. These include standard operating system files such as VSAM, BDAM, etc. Interfaces are handled by native access. Memory-resident information provides for very fast access to realtime information. Access is handled via services delivered by each product.

Multiple Platform Support

Repository Services utilize the Cooperative Processing and Distributed Database Services of CA90s to support multiple platform environments. Cooperative processing is based upon the CA Common Communication Interface (CAICCI) and distribution is provided through the use of CA distributed database technology.

Additional Services

Query and reporting services are necessary for any repository or dictionary. At the level of any given dictionary, native dictionary services, query facilities and reporting services are available. In addition to the Common Repository Interface, a form-based query and reporting facility is provided as part of Repository Services. Through nonprocedural, fill-in-the-blanks methods, users easily define forms that can be used as panels for online queries or as layouts for reporting purposes.

Event Notification Facility

The CA Event Notification Facility (CAIENF) is a unique software technology that represents a breakthrough in integration capabilities. It allows CA Enterprise Software Solutions, particularly those that rely on detailed interaction with an operating system such as Systems Management solutions, to achieve efficient portability and full integration goals as defined by CA90s.

The CA Event Notification Facility provides "event-" or object-oriented access to system and product activity within and across different environments. Applications, either systems- or business-related, monitor and post activity by "listening" for certain events or by issuing events themselves. Posting or "listening" for system activity via "events" is achieved through a single high-level programming interface that is common in format across multiple platforms and environments.

CA enterprise solutions can therefore access complex operating system and CA product activity data in a simple, consistent way, without each product requiring an intimate connection to the underlying operating system architecture.

For example, this powerful facility is implemented in CA-SCHEDULER, a component of CA-UNIPACK/APC. This production scheduling software no longer needs direct contact with MVS because CAIENF establishes the appropriate operating system intercepts. CA-ACF2 and CA-TOP SECRET, Computer Associates security solutions, provide good examples of the use of CAIENF to establish points of access control in CICS and DB2, insulating the solutions from changes within these operating environments.

Although CAIENF was specifically designed for CA Systems Management Software (because of their reliance on operating systems), other CA Enterprise Software Solutions can also take advantage of the information and services supplied by CAIENF. It is a powerful and easily applied tool for providing interoperability among all Enterprise Software Solutions, particularly among Systems Management Software and Business Applications Software. By issuing events on the one hand, and listening on the other, applications of all kinds can intercommunicate without the need for specialized interfaces, special protocols or "interface" programs. For example, by issuing scheduling-related events directly, a general ledger system can set criteria that a job scheduler can act upon programmatically, without any special interface.

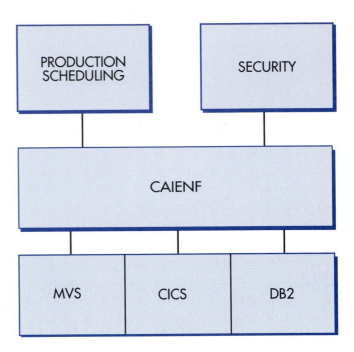

The CA Event Notification Facility, for example, notifies CA production scheduling software about MVS operating system activity and notifies CA security software about CICS and DB2 events.

CAIENF Services

CAIENF provides a wealth of valuable services that dramatically change the way CA solutions interact with the operating system and with each other. These new capabilities include:

A Single Point Of Control Between The Operating System And All CA Solutions

CAIENF will install, control and manage all operating system intercepts that are required by any CA enterprise solution, providing greater stability. This insulates the application from operating system mechanics and thus, from the usually time-consuming and effort-intensive tasks that result from operating system changes. In addition, the single point of control ensures a thorough quality test of each interface and eliminates any chance of conflicts with products that employ different interfacing techniques. Through CAIENF, enterprise solutions are insulated from any direct interrogation of operating system control blocks and from dependencies on operating system exits and intercept points.

A High-Level Interface For Information On Events

The high-level interface encourages information sharing across CA enterprise solutions and creates a new level of integration previously unattainable through traditional integration techniques. The CA enterprise solutions can request information about operating system or CA product events as logical processes rather than as operating system or product-specific requests. In addition, CAIENF gives each CA product a unique relational view of operating environment activity based on individual product requirements.

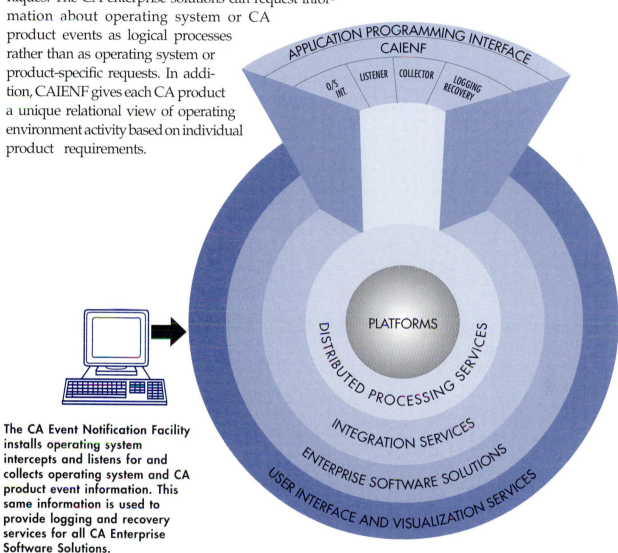

The CA Event Notification Facility installs operating system intercepts and listens for and collects operating system and CA product event information. This same information is used to provide logging and recovery services for all CA Enterprise Software Solutions.

For example, CAIENF provides platform-independent data requests such as "userid at signon" rather than the more traditional MVS dependent request that would be required in every application for "offset X'12' for a length of 8 in EBCDIC format in SMF record type 34 at IEFU83."

CAIENF speeds the development process for adding new functionality within CA solutions. With minimal coding effort, CA solutions can request information on operating system activity that is available through CAIENF. Before CAIENF, this information could only be accessed through intensive product-specific development activity.

CA solutions can also request information on activity generated by other CA solutions and act on the information, thereby extending automation capabilities . CAIENF extends this power even further by providing functionality across different operating systems and hardware platforms. For example, a job scheduler running on Digital VMS can "listen" for MVS-related job initiation events as criteria for managing VMS processes, and vice versa. Obviously, enterprise-wide communication capabilities through CAIENF offer tremendous benefits.

Notification Of Events

CAIENF provides CA enterprise solutions with the ability to "listen" for system or other CA Enterprise Software Solution events in a passive manner. CAIENF will automatically notify interested applications when the event occurs.

Exception conditions can also be detected by CAIENF and CA solutions can receive notification of events based on these exceptions.

CAIENF does not require any predefinition or registration of event points at a product level. Where needed, CA enterprise solutions can dynamically decide which events to process based on client needs and the specific CAIENF configuration.

For example, it may be desirable for a performance monitor to listen for specific operating system conditions. Using CAIENF, the application can choose from a list of all known event points, which will depend on the platform and the mix of vendor and CA software installed. This application can then automatically adapt to the installation of new CA solutions or the migration to other platforms.

In addition to regular events, which are passive and simply relate activity as it occurs, CAIENF supports the concept of "global" events, which allow applications to alter the flow of operating system activity. This capability is unique to CAIENF and is what permits true interoperability of systems products, such as tape management and security, that normally require extensive "hooks" specialized to a particular operating system. These "global hook techniques" are in use today in the global event handlers for CICS used by CA security software, CA-ACF2 and CA-TOP SECRET, to secure all CICS activity while remaining immune to changes in CICS. By using CAIENF, CA-ACF2 and CA-TOP SECRET secure all supported releases of CICS, using the same security code.

Central Checkpoint/Restart Facility For Recovery

CAIENF operates independently from any CA Enterprise Software Solution. When a CA product is inactive, for whatever reason, CAIENF continues to collect information on events. When the product is active again, it can request CAIENF to update it on all activity that has occurred since it was last active or, optionally, from a specific point in time. This allows the processing to continue as though it had not been interrupted.

High-Performance Asynchronous Processing

With CAIENF, product-related processing is not performed at the point of operating system intercept. This allows the operating system to service requests with minimal impact by CA enterprise solutions.

Dynamic Installation And Reconfiguration

CAIENF uses dynamic installation techniques for all operating system intercepts. Additionally, CAIENF employs the most appropriate interface technique for each operating system to ensure maximum efficiency. The advantage of this approach is extended to each CA solution that uses CAIENF to interface with the operating system.

Operating system intercepts are installed dynamically at CAIENF initiation without requiring IPLs or permanent modifications to operating system vendor code. In addition, critical CAIENF modules can be dynamically refreshed in order to apply (or remove) maintenance without impacting CA enterprise solutions that utilize CAIENF services.

Built-In Diagnostic Aids Which Simplify Problem Determination And Resolution

Diagnostics are produced automatically any time an error occurs and can be requested manually when appropriate. Because CAIENF is a common tool employed by CA enterprise solutions, it provides superior and more thorough diagnostic capabilities than are available in any individual solution. This enables CA solutions to be quickly and consistently supported in the event of any problem with operating system interfaces.

CAIENF Structure

CAIENF utilizes an object-oriented approach to information access. It allows enterprise solutions to access operating system objects in one of the following ways, according to the needs of the solution:

- *Event driven*—A condition (or series of conditions) occurs that triggers product action. User signon, data set access or operator messages are all examples of event-driven processes.
- *Realtime*—A product requests operating system data that is not related to an event, typically gathering statistical or configuration-specific data. Determining current system utilization, work load characteristics or system configuration are all examples of realtime data access.
- *Historical*—Details or summaries of system activity are presented to a product. "How long did his production batch job run last month?" is an example of historical data access.
- *Exceptions*—Events and realtime data elements can be verified against user- or product-supplied thresholds. Threshold violations can then be used to trigger subsequent product actions. For example, a performance monitor threshold exception could be "system utilization above 98 percent."

Benefits Of CAIENF

The use of CAIENF by Enterprise Software Solutions provides unique benefits to CA clients. No other vendor offers a technology that enables this level of functionality, integration and portability.

- *A new level of interoperability*—CAIENF allows CA Enterprise Software Solutions to "listen" for relevant events from the operating system and from other products and to take action based on this information. This is a unique capability that produces a previously unattainable degree of integration and communication among solutions.

- *Improved portability and consistency of CA solutions across operating environments*—By offering a high-level API for operating system event information, CAIENF eliminates much of what has traditionally been the most nonportable part of any software solution. CAIENF allows the bulk of most internal processing logic to be fully portable across operating environments at the source level. In addition, with CAIENF, the investment in processing logic can be preserved across platforms, eliminating the need for costly, time-consuming software redesign while ensuring consistency and maximum efficiency in all operating environments.

- *Improved overall performance, reliability and serviceability of CA software*—By insulating product code from operating system intercepts, CA enterprise solutions can run with minimal impact on the performance of the client system. Also, because CAIENF is a common service used by many CA products, all intercepts are highly optimized and benefit from the exploitation of the latest technology. For example CAIENF exploits the extended capabilities of IBM MVS/ESA operating environments thereby enabling all of CA Systems Management Software to fully utilize MVS/ESA functions. With CAIENF, individual CA solutions no longer require specific operating system intercepts or code that must execute in privileged modes.

- *Simplified integration capabilities for CA software*—CA software solutions can share the same information, offering a single solution for logging, recovery and reporting. Control options available within CAIENF allow management of all CA product information in a consistent manner.

- *Faster response to operating system changes*—All CA solutions will be able to quickly respond to operating system changes because CAIENF will be managing and controlling these intercepts directly, thereby insulating each individual CA solution from operating system changes.

- *Efficient exploitation of new technology*—As new operating system technologies are introduced, all CA solutions can quickly take advantage of new functionality through enhancements to CAIENF. This approach allows all CA solutions to benefit from new technologies simply by upgrading the CAIENF component.

Event Notification Facility And Other CA90s Services

CAIENF works closely both with the other components of the Integration Services layer and with other Service Layers to bring added functionality and benefits to the Enterprise Software Solutions.

- *Integration with Database Management Services*—CAIENF stores all parameter and event information in a shared relational database. This information can be retrieved through SQL or CAISQI routines if the requestor is authorized to do so.

- *Integration with dictionary technology*—All operating system objects available through the CAIENF API are dictionary-defined. CA enterprise solutions process CAIENF data elements at the data element level, allowing solution-specific type conversions or other reformatting to occur according to the dictionary definitions and the solution's needs.

Since CAIENF is dictionary-driven, defining new intercept points or data elements is simply a matter of updating the database. New solution requirements can typically be handled by a redefinition of existing data structures. In many cases, support for new solutions and features can be accomplished without the need for new code.

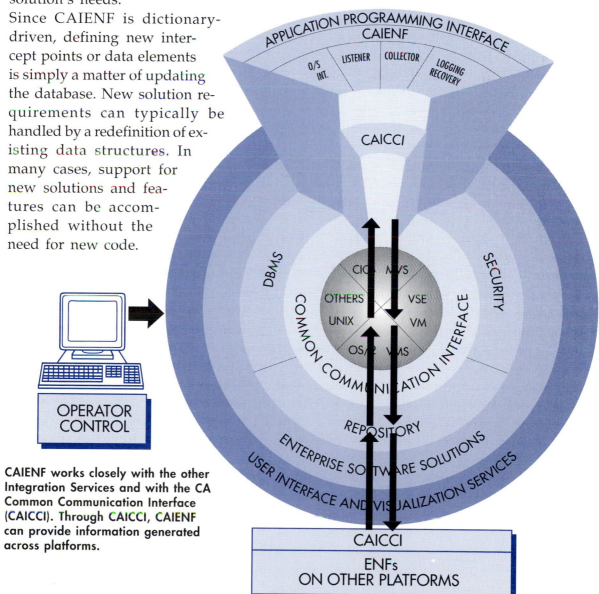

OPERATOR CONTROL

CAIENF works closely with the other Integration Services and with the CA Common Communication Interface (CAICCI). Through CAICCI, CAIENF can provide information generated across platforms.

- *Integration with Repository Services*—CAIENF will make use of the CA Common Repository Interface (CAICRI) for storage of product data requirements as well as for logging, recovery and reporting information.

  CAIENF relies on the Repository Services for CA solution control parameters, logging of system events and logging of CA solution events through entity-relationship technology. All CA solutions will continue to use CAIENF for the logging of product activity. CAIENF data recorded through Repository Services will be made available to CA solutions through the standard CAIENF API, by coding CAICRI calls or by SQL statements targeted directly at the CAIENF database.

- *Integration with security*—CAIENF controls the setting of events and access to recorded events through the CA Standard Security Facility (CAISSF). Only specifically authorized CA solutions and routines can define new events or retrieve information stored within the CAIENF database.

- *Integration with standard communications*—CAIENF uses CAICCI communications facilities to allow solutions to process operating system objects across network nodes. Operating system events and realtime data may be obtained using CAICCI from any system that is connected, including heterogeneous platforms.

  Solutions request cross-operating system objects by standard CAIENF API calls so that no special networking support is needed within the solutions in order for them to benefit from these features.

Standard Security Facility

A long-standing Computer Associates strategic policy has been to integrate CA security solutions with all other CA enterprise solutions. CA90s reinforces this direction by including security as a standard service component.

The CA Standard Security Facility (CAISSF) provides a single external security mechanism for controlling and monitoring access to all system and application resources and processes. It interacts directly with CA's industry-leading security solutions, CA-ACF2 and CA-TOP SECRET, and alternatively supports platform-specific security mechanisms where appropriate.

CAISSF is a service unique to CA90s. No other architecture or vendor describes security as an integrated component for controlling access to all system and solution-related information and processing throughout the enterprise.

The use of a single security mechanism, such as CAISSF, ensures that all CA Enterprise Software Solutions benefit from the comprehensive functions available through CA security solutions. Additionally, security administration is simplified because all administrative functions are provided through the same security facilities. These security facilities also make it possible to distribute security administration to multiple platforms, if required.

CAISSF supplies a standard API to support different external security mechanisms across different operating system platforms. This standardization significantly improves the portability of enterprise solutions across these platforms.

CAISSF is used by both the CA enterprise solutions and the components of CA90s Service Layers for single-point user signon, resource access control, process use control, and recording and monitoring of violation activity.

CAISSF is already utilized by many CA enterprise solutions. For example, the CA Systems Management solutions that already use CAISSF include CA-SCHEDULER, CA-7, CA-APCDOC, CA-JARS, CA-VMAN, CA-ASM2, CA-DYNAM/TLMS and CA-1, to cite just a few. CA Information Management solutions that use CAISSF include CA-IDEAL, CA-LIBRARIAN, CA-IDMS/DC, CA-ROSCOE, CA-VOLLIE and others. In addition, CAISSF is utilized by the CA Masterpiece suite of Business Applications solutions.

CA90s services also use CAISSF. For example, the CA Database Management Services and systems such as CA-DATACOM/DB and CA-IDMS/DB use CAISSF. Additionally, the CA Event Notification Facility (CAIENF) and the CA Common Communication Interface (CAICCI) use CAISSF to control access to processes and information.

CA will explicitly use CAISSF external security for all CA solutions and services as new releases become available.

CAISSF is currently utilized on multiple operating system platforms including IBM MVS, VSE and VM, and will be extended to additional IBM and non-IBM platforms as needed.

The CA Standard Security Facility is already well integrated into many CA Enterprise Software Solutions and other CA90s services.

CAISSF Components

CAISSF consists of the following components:

• A security driver that processes a general platform-independent API that combines the requirements/features of both CA-ACF2 and CA-TOP SECRET.

• A CA-ACF2 translator to change the CA-ACF2 return codes and access levels into CAISSF format.

• A CA-TOP SECRET translator to change the CA-TOP SECRET return codes and access levels into CAISSF format.

• A non-CA product exit that is called for any operation for which a non-CA compatible security mechanism is found.

The CA Standard Security Facility provides integration with CA-ACF2, CA-TOP SECRET and non-CA platform-specific external security mechanisms.

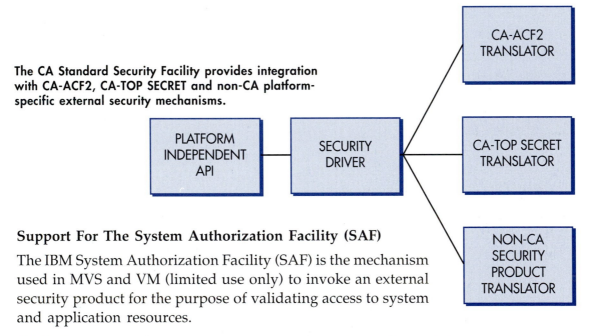

Support For The System Authorization Facility (SAF)

The IBM System Authorization Facility (SAF) is the mechanism used in MVS and VM (limited use only) to invoke an external security product for the purpose of validating access to system and application resources.

CAISSF and CA security products will support all SAF calls made by operating system components. These calls will be handled in the most appropriate manner for CA-ACF2 and CA-TOP SECRET.

However, CAISSF extends security service beyond SAF. Whereas SAF is only available for the MVS and VM operating systems (and the SAF interfaces for these two environments are not compatible), CAISSF currently supports MVS, VSE and VM and is being extended to many other platforms as well. Additionally, CAISSF is designed to take advantage of the full functionality of CA-ACF2 and CA-TOP SECRET. SAF-compatible or other hardware vendor-specific products are supported with only a subset of CAISSF functions due to the limited capabilities of SAF.

When processing via CAISSF, it is not necessary for the application to adjust the calls for the particular security system or operating system. CAISSF will do the necessary interpretation.

CAISSF delivers the following additional features:

- The same API is used in all operating systems. This allows for source level transportability across these operating systems.
- A status function returns information stating which CA security product is active. It also indicates if a hardware vendor-specific product is installed.
- A generic signon interface returns the address of a "user identification token" to identify the user's security environment and appropriate messages.
- A generic signoff interface utilizes the security environment token from the signon function.
- A generic resource-checking interface provides return codes and messages for either CA security system. Return codes and their meanings are standardized to eliminate any need for multiple interpretation.
- Dynamic loading of the CAISSF module eliminates the need for linking the module or locating it via hard anchor points.
- A simple API-driven interface for all functions is provided. Dynamic loading of the interface is integral to the API.

Security Development Guidelines

CA has published strict security guidelines to which each CA Enterprise Software Solution must adhere. For example:

- Signon—If a CA solution requires signon the CA solution will use CAISSF to extract user information for signon purposes. In this way, the signon to authorized applications is transparent to the user. Additionally, this approach provides single-point registration for the security administrator, who no longer has to deal with internal security tables or files.

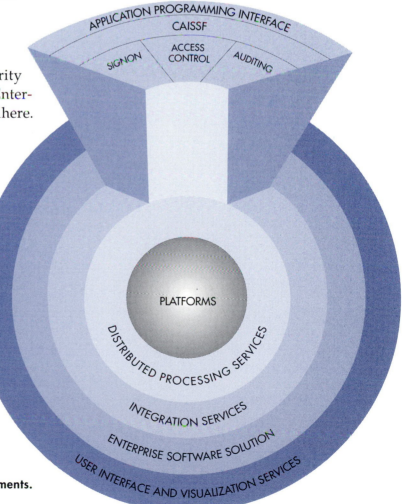

CAISSF supports all CA Enterprise Software Solution security requirements.

- Resource and process access control—All appropriate resources and processes are definable to the CA security solutions so that they can be controlled through normal standard security mechanisms.
- Auditing—All auditing of resource access and recording of violations will be handled by the security component. This will allow security administrators to monitor user activity through a single-point facility.

If a CA enterprise solution, such as Masterpiece, currently provides an internal security facility, that facility can be maintained as an option based on CA client requirements. However, all functionality of the internal security will be mirrored through the external security interface so that CA clients have the option of completely replacing the internal security with external security.

B1 Level Functionality

A major priority for security software development is the inclusion of functions that will allow CA security solutions to meet the B1 level of trust as set forth by the National Computer Security Center (NCSC). These requirements are defined in "Department of Defense Trusted Computer System Evaluation Criteria" (DoD 5200.28-STD), better known as the Orange Book.

The National Computer Security Center was formed to encourage the availability of "trusted" computer systems for those installations that need to process sensitive or classified data. The NCSC is also charged with evaluating such systems to determine what level of trust is met. A vendor such as CA indicates to the NCSC that it wishes a product to be evaluated. The NCSC designates a project, under which the vendor performs the necessary development, and then the NCSC formally evaluates the resulting system. This culminates in a statement from the NCSC indicating the criteria that are met and the level of trust that is satisfied. The product then is placed on the Evaluated Products List if it meets the necessary requirements.

To date, CA security solutions have already been evaluated at the C2 level of trust and were placed on the Evaluated Products List. Currently CA-ACF2 MVS and CA-TOP SECRET MVS are under evaluation for a B1 rating as shown below.

CA security solutions are evaluated at various levels of trust by the National Computer Security Center.

PRODUCT	C2	B1
CA-ACF2 MVS	Rating Received AUG. 1984	Under Evaluation
CA-TOP SECRET MVS	Rating Received APR. 1985	Under Evaluation
CA-ACF2 VM	Rating Received SEPT. 1987	
CA-TOP SECRET VM	Filed For Evaluation	

CA is making these same four products, listed in the table, certifiable at the B1 level of trust.

The differences between the C2 and B1 levels of trust can be explained as follows: Products evaluated at the C2 level of trust provide discretionary access control or the ability to control access on a "need to know" basis. These systems effect the separation of users and data and provide a way to place access limitations on a specific user. C2 systems provide greater discretionary control and provide for individual user accountability through logon identification, auditing of events that are related to security issues, and the isolation of the system resources so they are subject to the identification and auditing features. Discretionary Access Control (DAC) is the currently used method in CA security products.

Products that meet the B1 level of trust provide Mandatory Access Control (MAC) based on classification of users and sensitivity labeling of objects or data. This is the main additional requirement for B1 class systems over C2 class systems. B1 class systems are concerned with "secrecy" of information rather than "need to know." CA B1 security solutions will provide classification and labeling of users and objects and will enforce mandatory access control based on these sensitivity labels.

MAC will be made available to all CA enterprise solutions through the use of CAISSF. MAC may also be used where it is appropriate to the individual application. For example, the NCSC is proposing a Trusted Database Interpretation (TDI) of the Orange Book which will include both DAC and MAC. When it is appropriate for CA database management solutions to incorporate this level of security, Computer Associates will be able to do so quickly and easily through CAISSF.

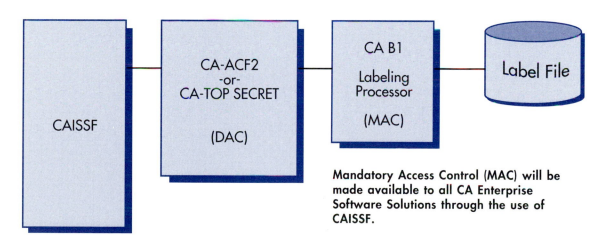

Mandatory Access Control (MAC) will be made available to all CA Enterprise Software Solutions through the use of CAISSF.

Benefits Of CAISSF

A single image of security implemented across many otherwise disparate hardware environments brings many benefits in terms of manageability:

- *Global control of each user*—Through management of each user as a unique entity, central or local control of users may be accomplished in a manner that maintains security, integrity and accountability in accordance with corporate standards and direction. Also, each user can identify himself as a single entity and manage his password accordingly, regardless of hardware platform.

- *Global enforcement*—With cross-system and cross-vendor communication, CA software will be able to react to any attempt to gain unauthorized access across all platforms. This will prevent "hacker" attacks where an individual goes after the same account in many locations until successful.

- *Minimal impact on business activity*—CA security solutions are, and will continue to be, positioned for selective implementation and local control of access wherever desirable from a corporate standpoint.

- *Protection of investments in education*—With global security control available through CAISSF, investments made in training personnel in the use of CA security solutions are protected because expertise can be directly applied to each new addition of CA security controls, resources or platforms. CA security maintains a common look, feel and terminology for all applications, and eliminates the problems of maintaining dissimilar security systems, as is the case even within the IBM security offerings across disparate operating system platforms.

- *Increased auditability and accountability*—With a common platform for all auditing activity, enforcement and accountability can be ensured for the first time. In addition, the use of common CA services for reporting minimizes training requirements and reduces the likelihood of errors in analysis due to unfamiliarity with a particular platform.

- *Enhanced control and productivity through integration*—Complete and tight security integration with each CA enterprise solution provides easy and consistent control of security at a very detailed level. The use of CA90s security services by each CA solution is specified by a CA corporate security standard to ensure consistency of both function and appearance across product lines and operating system platforms.

Application Services

Application Services provide Enterprise Software Solutions with a wealth of useful capabilities. Many of the functions represent advanced technological developments available to clients only from Computer Associates. Other capabilities are more widely available, but gain significant value and added functionality from being accessible to all Enterprise Software Solutions through the Integration Services layer. In addition, many of the Application Services are available as standalone functions for use by CA clients.

Application Services include *single-point signon* and *single-point user registration* capabilities, *decision support* tools, *project management* solutions, *change management* functions, *expert systems* capabilities, a *product validation interface, C runtime* facilities, common *installation and maintenance* facilities, and common *service and support* functions.

In many instances, the various Application Services utilize other components of the CA90s Service Layers for standard internal functions. For example, CA-UNISERVICE/II, an automated service and support solution for all CA enterprise software, uses the CA Common Communication Interface (Distributed Processing Services layer) to handle PC-to-mainframe communications requirements.

The CA90s strategy for Application Services calls for improving the usefulness and portability of these services. They will then be made available on additional platforms to provide standard services to all CA enterprise solutions as these solutions are ported to new environments.

CA Application Services provide many standard end-user functions to CA clients when integrated with CA Enterprise Software Solutions.

Single-Point Signon

As enterprise solutions become available on multiple operating systems and multiple hardware platforms, they bring with them the requirement for users to identify themselves to the system on which they will work. In some cases, this identification is required for multiple systems on the same platform.

To address this growing need, CA has introduced the concept of single-point signon. This concept significantly simplifies the process of seamlessly linking heterogeneous platforms.

Single-point signon allows users to identify themselves at one point in the network, without requiring additional signons when accessing individual applications, no matter where those applications reside. Technology transparent to users handles the internal signons required when each new application is accessed by propagating to each application user IDs (or an alias if the ID is different on another platform) and passwords (or a token if a more secure signon process is required).

Password changes are also managed at this single point of network entry and can be propagated to any platform-specific security databases that require this information in order to validate the signons. Network entry validation at a single point of entry can also be performed for extended user authentication devices (biometrics, smart cards, etc.) to further ensure that users are accurately identified.

Single-point signon provides important benefits to organizations. End users need to signon only once with a single ID and password. This not only simplifies and speeds up the signon process, but improves security as well. By requiring end users to re-member only one ID and password, the risk of compromising security by users who write down difficult-to-remember IDs and passwords is eliminated. In addition, a single point of entry becomes a single point of control, further securing access to the corporate network.

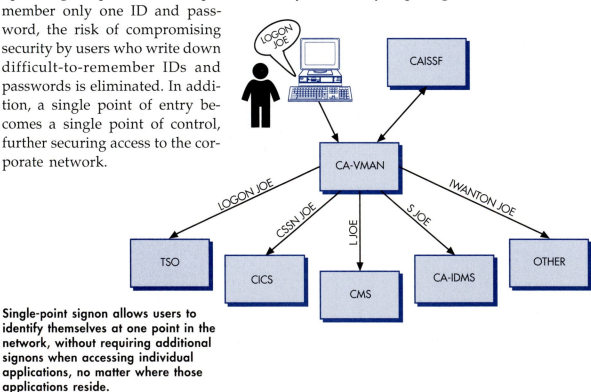

Single-point signon allows users to identify themselves at one point in the network, without requiring additional signons when accessing individual applications, no matter where those applications reside.

Single-Point User Registration

Due to the complexity of today's information processing operations, registering users with the proper applications is becoming a very time-consuming task and frequently a decentralized function. The combinations of applications and system facilities spread across multiple operating systems that require user registration can seem limitless. When users request access to an application, they must first be given access to the operating node, then access to the application. The same steps must be followed in reverse order to delete a user from the system.

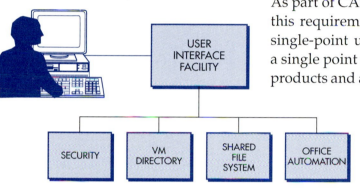

As part of CA90s, Computer Associates is addressing this requirement with a new application service for single-point user registration. This feature provides a single point of user registration for CA and non-CA products and applications thereby simplifying the administration and increasing the accuracy of user registration.

Single-point user registration implemented in an IBM VM environment.

Decision Support

A broad range of decision support tools are provided by Application Services to address the multiplatform financial planning, modeling, reporting and spreadsheet needs of CA clients.

For example, CA provides advanced spreadsheet functionality that spans mainframe, midrange and desktop platforms, in addition to enabling cooperative desktop processing with access to mainframe information. SuperCalc and CA-SuperCalc/VAX, leading spreadsheet solutions, can also access relational databases directly, a simple matter since the row-and-column format that is standard for spreadsheets is directly analogous to relational tables.

CA decision support tools transform data generated from CA Enterprise Software Solutions into useful information for effective decision making.

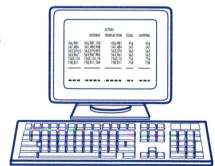

CA-Compete!, operating with a graphical user interface under Windows, adds true multidimensional data viewing, modeling and reporting to the fundamental spreadsheet paradigm. With simple click, drag and drop operations with a mouse, the user can take different perspectives on data, up to 12 dimensions; through a direct link with the Window-based query facility CA-Compete! provides invaluable insight into mainframe database information.

Project Management

Today, CA provides a wide range of project management solutions ranging from desktop-to-midrange-to-mainframe oriented solutions, with the ability to transfer files among them. CA will continue to build upon these technologies and, as part of the Integration Services layer of CA90s, will make them an integral part of CA enterprise solutions where appropriate.

The advantages of consistent techniques and methods of project management have become increasingly important in many organizations as IS executives realize that optimizing resources, costs and schedules can mean the difference between the failure and success of application development projects.

Project management tools from CA support an increasingly wide range of processing platforms to enable users to interact using a consistent, familiar interface. The tools

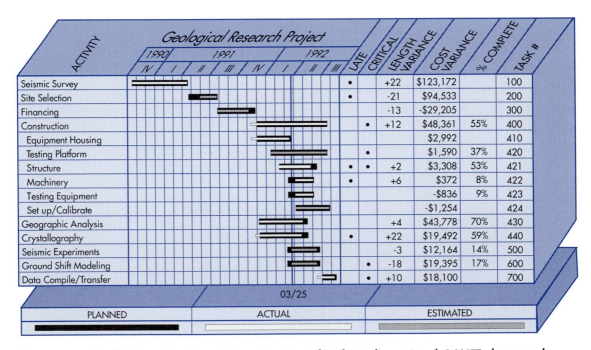

As an example of CA project management services, this three-dimensional GANTT chart can be created on a mainframe or midrange platform or through connectivity with desktop systems.

provide a graphical user interface under Windows, while maintaining a consistent look-and-feel with the character-based interfaces on other platforms. Decentralized planning and consolidation facilities are also provided. In addition, the new constructs and methods employed by CASE methodologies such as rapid prototyping and concept evaluation are included.

Integration with other CA90s services will enable direct connectivity of project management tools to CA Database Management Services and Repository Services for streamlined import/export of project-related information.

Change Management

As the complexity of information processing grows, so does the importance and need for effective change management. Change management is a focal point for all data center activities and should be integrated with any software that can alter the information processing configuration throughout the enterprise.

CA90s recognizes the importance of effective enterprise-wide change management and therefore provides Application Services to handle the management of change driven by any CA software. In conjunction with CA Repository Services, through which all change objects are defined, and CA solutions, which manage the objects, the Change Management Service manages and controls change requests.

This service allows all changes to the information processing operation (hardware, software, user profiles, etc.) to be recorded, approved and implemented in a consistent fashion. It further provides information about any change's impact on other objects and ensures that the change is thoroughly understood before it is scheduled for implementation.

The Change Management Service, in conjunction with Repository Services (to define change objects) and CA solutions (to manage change objects), control the change request process.

Expert Systems

CA90s promotes the use of expert systems as an effective means of automating solutions to complex business problems. With expert systems, the knowledge of an organization's experts, regardless of their field of expertise, can be easily captured and made available to other resources in the enterprise.

This archived expertise can be used as a tool for teaching new personnel and encouraging consistency in decisions that are made. Experienced personnel can be freed up to concentrate on the significant changes and variations within the enterprise while expert systems provide advice on recurring problem situations.

An example of expert systems technology is CA-DB:EXPERT. As part of the Integration Services layer of CA90s, this technology provides CA enterprise solutions with a tool for automating the decision-making processes inherent in enterprise operations, improving diagnostic capabilities through the use of embedded expert systems, reducing setup and implementation time for each CA solution, capturing and distributing expertise and providing an interface to new areas such as voice technology.

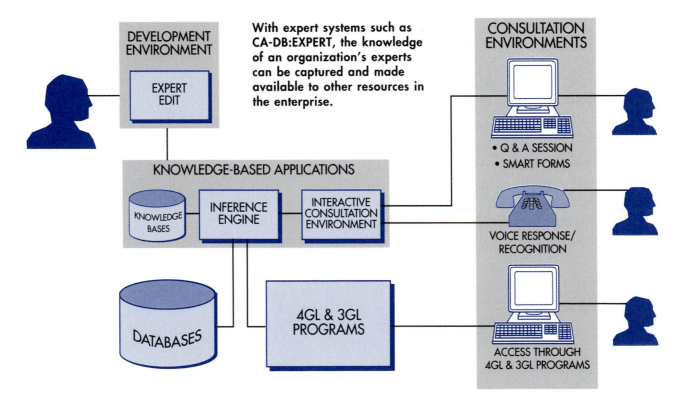

Product Validation Interface

CA90s promotes integrity of CA product installation through the use of the unique CA Product Validation Interface (CAIPVI). This capability benefits clients immeasurably by providing an installation verification service for CA and other vendor software to ensure that enterprise solutions are correctly installed and to ensure runtime integrity.

This technology is already available as part of CA-EXAMINE, Computer Associates operating system audit and integrity software.

CAIPVI allows software developers to describe their products in an encrypted CA Product Description Module (CAIPDM) that is shipped with the vendor-supplied product. When the product is installed at a client site, the Product Validation Interface will use the information as described in the CAIPDM to verify that the product is correctly installed and to ensure runtime integrity.

While CAIPVI was originally developed for use with CA software, this unique technology can be used to verify the integrity of any product.

Currently, CAIPVI supports user SVCs and system exits, common points where the integrity of the software might be compromised. CAIPVI also recognizes product interfaces in other areas such as I/O appendages, PPT, TSO APF commands, subsystems and SMF records.

As new releases of CA products are made available, CAIPVI will automatically recognize new CAIPDMs as they appear and will verify the installation of the associated products. This will allow CA clients to have a high level of assurance that CA software is installed as intended and is not being compromised.

Through the CA Product Validation Interface, CA-EXAMINE verifies that CA software is correctly installed in the operating system.

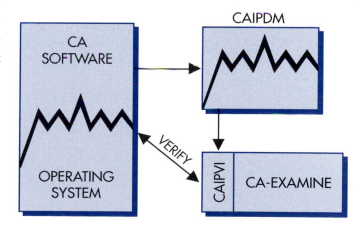

C Runtime Services

The C Runtime Services are unique technologies available only through CA90s. These facilities bring the portability, software development simplicity, maintenance ease and comprehensive documentation capabilities of the C language, commonly found in PC environments, to mainframe software. Through CA90s C Runtime facilities, the power of the C language is available to mainframe systems management, database and applications software.

The C Runtime Services consist of a high-quality C compiler, runtime library, a fully integrated development environment including debugging facilities, testing and quality assurance capabilities, support for CA90s services including the User Interface Management Services of CA90s, and support for CA Extended SQL.

Computer Associates C compiler and runtime library are an integral part of CA90s Enterprise Software Solutions and feature high levels of ANSI compatibility, and object compatibility across MVS, VSE and VM. The C Runtime compiler generates fully reentrant, 31-bit code, enabling the application to fully exploit the platforms on which it runs such as MVS/XA or ESA environments.

Examples of the mainframe environments that are supported by the C Runtime Services include batch, TSO, CICS, CMS, IMS/DC, CA-IDMS/DC and CA-ROSCOE. Other environments, such as desktop and VAX midrange systems, use native C compilers with extensions for CA90s service APIs when required.

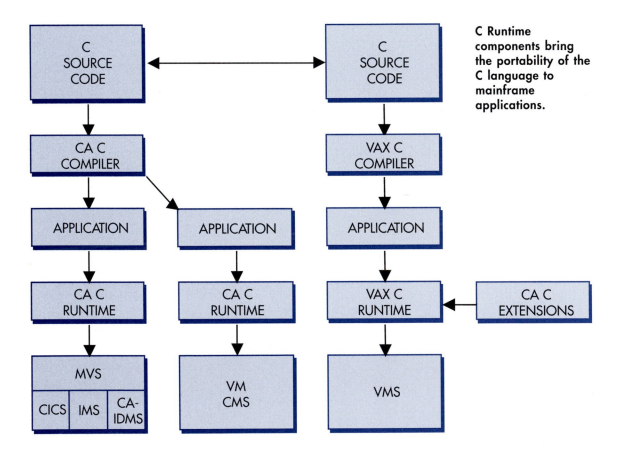

C Runtime components bring the portability of the C language to mainframe applications.

Installation And Maintenance

The effective installation and maintenance of each enterprise solution and its associated service components is critical to the successful use of software solutions. CA introduced the concept of "common components" in CA products many years ago with the use of standard functions, such as dynamic installation routines.

With CA90s and Enterprise Software Solutions' reliance on the many common components of the Service Layers, effective installation management services have become essential requirements.

For example, when several CA solutions use the Event Notification Facility (CAIENF), installation management services ensure that CAIENF is properly installed when the first CA solution that relies on it is installed. Thereafter, installation management services ensure that CAIENF is appropriately notified and is not adversely affected when more CA solutions are added.

An example of CA Installation and Maintenance services that is already in use is CA-ACTIVATOR. This is a menu-driven common service application that already provides an interactive product installation and maintenance facility. This automated service eliminates misdefined installation parameters, conflicting product options, incorrectly assigned libraries and other costly difficulties inherent in manual installation procedures. It further manages the sharing of common components among all CA solutions that utilize them. CA-ACTIVATOR will continue to be kept current with the installation and maintenance requirements of new CA90s technology as it is introduced.

CA90s Installation and Maintenance Services support the utilization of installation standards that are already in wide use. An example of this is IBM's SMP/E, which is the basis for installation and maintenance of IBM MVS products.

In addition, for installation and maintenance as well as for regular use of CA solutions, CA-DOCVIEW provides online viewing of product documentation with comprehensive facilities for indexed search and navigation.

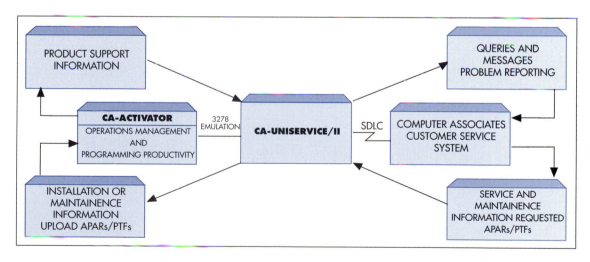

CA90s provides standard Installation and Maintenance Services through CA-ACTIVATOR and automated Service and Support facilities through CA-UNISERVICE/II for all CA Enterprise Software Solutions.

Service And Support

Each CA Enterprise Software Solution is supported by common service and support facilities to provide standard services to CA clients. This Application Service provides a broad range of advanced online service, support and training facilities that are engineered to provide reliability, availability and serviceability to a client data center.

These standard facilities are already available to clients in CA-UNISERVICE/II, an interactive application that links the CA internal client support system with individual client sites. The CA Common Communication Interface (CAICCI) is used as the communications software that allows clients to establish connectivity through a CA-supplied PC workstation, or additionally, through any 3270 terminal with access to CA-ACTIVATOR at the client installation.

The services available to clients through this service and support facility include:

• Access to product support and general information
• Direct interaction with CA technical support staff through electronic mail facilities
• Access to the CA APAR/PTF database for viewing and, alternatively, retrieval of current product fixes
• Access to the CA Product Information Bulletin Board
• Access to the Online Request Desk to request product enhancement information
• Access to the Order Desk to facilitate ordering of manuals, video training material and workbooks
• Training through PC-based tutorials

In addition, another new facility, known as SHADOW, enables CA Customer Service technicians to actually link to client's systems and view the contents of their terminal, and if desired, obtain control in order to diagnose the problem.

Summary

Through the layered design of CA90s and the advanced technology incorporated in the Integration Services layer, Computer Associates breaks through the traditional limitations of product integration to deliver a new level of software interoperability.

Enterprises are no longer faced with the confusion caused by "multiple versions of the truth," a common situation that arises from the presence of multiple data sources and nonintegrated software systems. Through CA90s Integration Services, enterprises move significantly closer to achieving a single point of information management, interoperability of software solutions and security that ensures the accuracy, availability and integrity of enterprise-wide information even across multi-vendor, multi-operating system platforms.

Through CA90s Integration Services, enterprises gain control of their information systems and can utilize them effectively as strategic business tools.

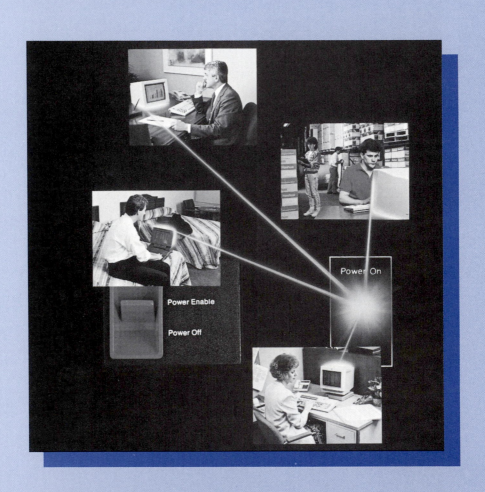

CHAPTER 5

Distributed Processing Services

In a traditional, centralized environment, all processing (such as user interfacing, application logic and database management) is performed on the same system, whether it is a mainframe, midrange or PC. A decentralized processing environment allows the distribution of both processing and information to appropriate platforms.

Distributed processing capabilities will become more critical to enterprises' overall success as they attempt to compete effectively in global markets. Distributing information and applications across a variety of computing environments allows more informed and timely decision making to take place closer to the actual local business unit.

In addition, distributed processing capabilities give enterprises the flexibility to select hardware platforms that offer the best price/performance and that are sized to the tasks being performed. This allows enterprises to take maximum advantage of the often underutilized power available in the growing number of workstations and desktop systems.

However, the only way enterprises can attain these benefits and effectively manage distributed processing is by providing enterprise-wide distribution of information and applications while ensuring the complete integrity and uniform use of the information. Without this comprehensive management control, enterprises are faced with a multitude of computing systems that process and deliver unreliable and inconsistent information again presenting "multiple versions of the truth."

Only Computer Associates provides unrivaled support for all forms of distributed processing, as well as the essential control capabilities for ensuring the integrity of the distributed information and applications.

CA Enterprise Software Solutions utilize the Distributed Processing Services layer of CA90s to achieve this functionality. The standard services of this layer support the different configurations of distribution, grouped into two categories:

- *Cooperative Processing*—where *processing* is distributed to different systems for optimal responsiveness, exploitation of the best price/performance ratio for low-volume and high-volume processing, optimal network traffic, and realistic security and control. The Cooperative Processing Services of CA90s provide support for application-to-application cooperative processing and for client-server architectures.

- *Database Server and Distributed Database*—where *information* is available through global access and centralized control or is distributed to different systems for local control and responsiveness. These two forms of distributed information are also closely integrated with the Database Management Services of CA90s.

In addition, the Distributed Processing Services layer includes the *CA Common Communication Interface (CAICCI)* which standardizes communication with connectivity software and enables CA Enterprise Software Solutions to span multi-platform environments.

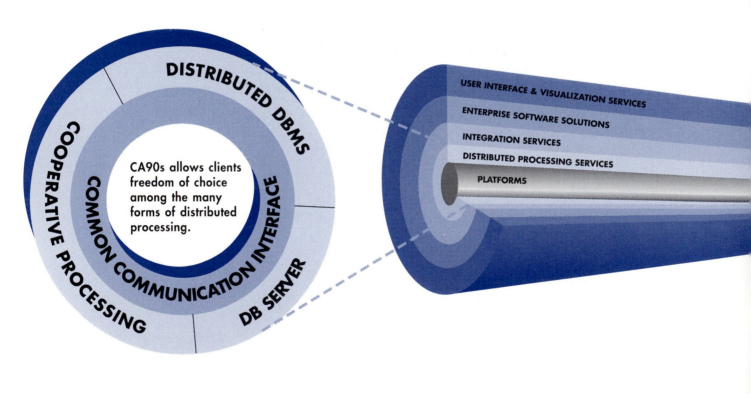

Cooperative Processing

Cooperative processing is used increasingly by enterprises to take advantage of the low-cost processing power provided by desktop and midrange systems, to improve user interfaces through the responsiveness and graphical capabilities of desktop workstations, to reduce network traffic by providing local processing where it is needed and to integrate operations across remote parts of the enterprise.

While the underlying communications technology is the same, it is helpful to consider the main configurations of cooperative processing as separate implementations, with different enabling technologies provided by the Distributed Processing Services of CA90s. The main categories are application-to-application cooperative processing and client-server configurations.

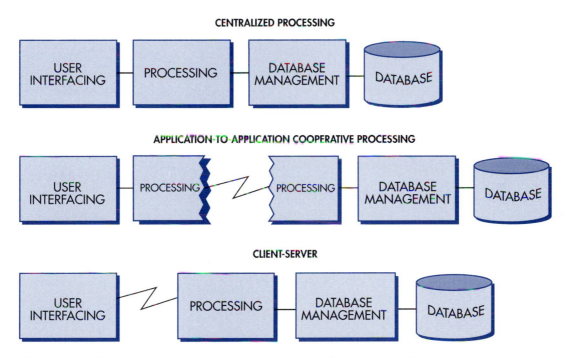

The main configurations of cooperative processing, application-to-application cooperative processing and client-server provide greater flexibility than traditional, centralized processing.

Application-to-application cooperative processing allows enterprise solutions to communicate as partners. For example, CA security solutions, CA-ACF2 and CA-TOP SECRET, integrate individual security processes across MVS and VMS platforms.

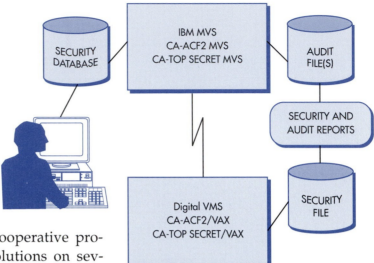

Application-to-application cooperative processing allows enterprise solutions on several systems, each doing application-level processing, to cooperate as partners in achieving a desired function. (The term "peer-to-peer" is often used to describe this partnership.) In some cases, the local systems are complete applications in their own right, each doing its own job, all cooperating toward a higher goal. In other cases, the whole distributed system is considered the application, with each local environment merely a component of the whole. In either case, application-to-application cooperative processing involves application logic sending application-level information over the network.

For example, several Computer Associates security solutions, available on IBM mainframes and Digital VAX systems, utilize the Distributed Processing Services layer to act in tandem to integrate individual security processes on the different platforms. This eases security administration and improves control of security in decentralized organizations.

Another form of cooperative processing, the client-server architecture, involves application logic on one system requesting a standard service on another. While the communication technology and processes are the same, client-server differs from application-to-application in that one side of the cooperation is a standard service without application-specific logic, and the information communicated is not application specific. There is no peer-level relationship. One side requests a service, the other side is subordinate and delivers the service.

For example, user interfacing, data validation and help may be downloaded to a PC as a service, giving an application relying on the "industrial strength" processing capabilities of a mainframe the immediacy of response and improved productivity of a desktop workstation. Examples of this implementation are already in use in CA-MASTERSTATION (a component of CA Financial Management Software) and CA-DATAQUERY/PC (a component of CA Information Management Software).

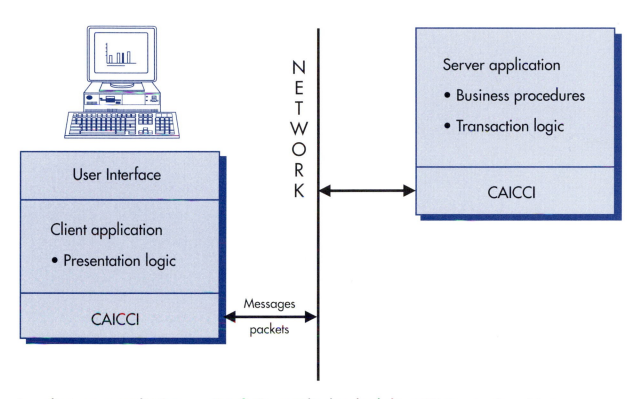

In a client-server application, user interfacing may be downloaded to a PC as a service, giving an application relying on the "industrial strength" processing capabilities of a mainframe the immediacy of response and improved productivity of a desktop workstation.

The CA90s Cooperative Processing Services provide enabling technology including message transfer services and remote procedure call capabilities that simplify the implementation of client-server architectures as well as application-to-application cooperative processing. These services are also available to CA clients through CA application development tools, allowing CA clients to build their own distributed applications with the same configurations that were discussed for CA solutions. High-level language interfaces simplify the development of these applications without requiring the use of assembly-level code or extensive communications expertise. An example of this technology is provided in CA application development solutions such as CA-ADS, CA-ADS/PC and CA-DB:GENERATOR/PC.

Database Server

CA database server technology allows remote access and centralized database management of a multi-user database, and is most often applied to desktop systems. Traditionally, desktop databases are single-user databases. Desktop systems can now take advantage of shared data with other desktop systems through LANs connecting them to a database server. Through the use of database servers, desktop systems can also share information with midrange and mainframe systems.

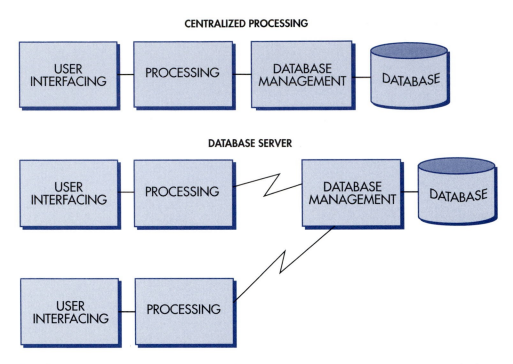

CENTRALIZED PROCESSING

| USER INTERFACING | PROCESSING | DATABASE MANAGEMENT | DATABASE |

DATABASE SERVER

Database server technology allows desktop systems to share data with other desktop systems, a significant improvement over the traditional single-user database implementations.

Database servers provide enterprises with improved integration of information processing components as well as an effective means of managing and controlling the multiple users of the database through central points of update and control. Data integrity is ensured because, regardless of the number of users, there is a single point of control, a single point of update and a single point of audit.

The shared multi-user environment made possible by database servers supports data dictionary access in addition to database management services, further extending the benefits of shared databases.

CA database server technology has been implemented in many CA enterprise solutions on many platforms. For example, CA-DATACOM/DB and CA-IDMS/DB currently provide database server technology on mainframe platforms; CA-IDMS/PC and CA-DATACOM/PC provide it for Local Area Network (LAN) implementations, and CA-DB/VAX and CA-DB/UNIX provide it for VMS and UNIX environments as well as for PC/LAN environments.

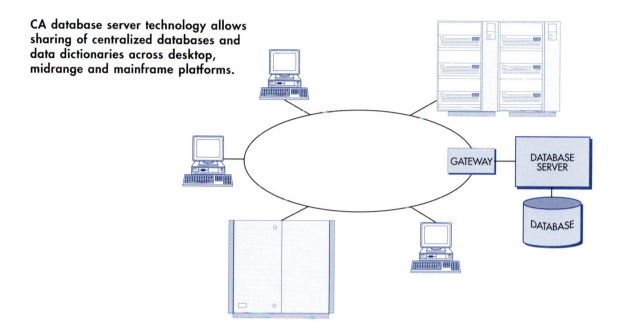

CA database server technology allows sharing of centralized databases and data dictionaries across desktop, midrange and mainframe platforms.

Distributed Database

Distributed database technology allows software solutions to access information without regard for the physical location of the data, while ensuring that integrity and effective transaction management are maintained. The database could be local, remote or even distributed across several systems. A good example of CA distributed database technology that is currently utilized by CA clients is CA-DB:STAR.

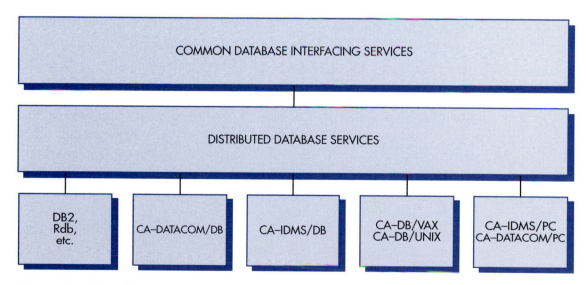

CA Distributed Database Services provide the technology to access CA databases as well as other vendor database management systems.

Distributed databases enable organizations to determine the physical location of the database based on performance and environmental conditions. For example, local processing of transactions can improve performance and response time. In addition, because of the transparency to the application programmer, the database administrator can optimize performance by reconfiguring the database without requiring application changes.

With CA distributed database technology, information appears to end users as if the distributed database were a single, local database. A benefit of distributed database technology is that local access to information needed by end users is not affected if network connections are down.

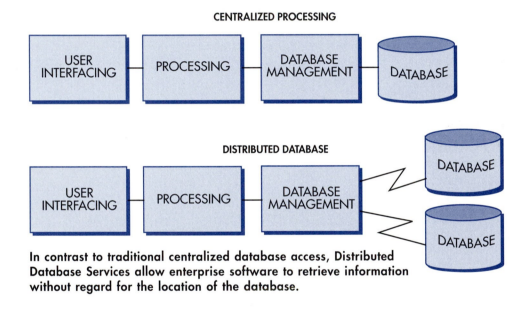

CENTRALIZED PROCESSING

DISTRIBUTED DATABASE

In contrast to traditional centralized database access, Distributed Database Services allow enterprise software to retrieve information without regard for the location of the database.

CA Distributed Database Services provide:

- *Location transparency*—Distributed database capabilities permit applications to access and update distributed data as if it were stored locally in a single database. No special application code is required. Distributed Database Services allow the transparent distribution of data among multiple mainframe computers, midrange computers, LAN servers, and desktop systems.

  Through the use of CA90s Distributed Database Services, users can access and update data easily without having to know its actual site location. Users are not required to be familiar with network links or to know how data is actually routed through the network. The technical complexities associated with remote data access are completely transparent to the application programmer and, ultimately, to the end user.

- *Partition transparency*—With CA Distributed Database Services, data can be horizontally partitioned (subdivided) so that each subdivision can be located according to operational or economic efficiencies. For example, customer information can be partitioned according to sales office and distributed to the local office. Whether the subdivisions are local or remote is transparent to the program, which operates unchanged regardless of whether the data is partitioned or not.

- *Replication transparency*—Multiple copies, or replicas, of data can be created. The CA Distributed Database Services automatically ensure that updates to any replicated data are posted automatically to all other copies of the database. Access speed, data availability, and physical safety factors are provided by the distributed database replication facility.

- *Integrity control (two-phase commit)*—CA Distributed Database Services, not the user, are responsible for maintaining the integrity of replicated and partitioned data even when the updates of a logical unit of work span multiple locations or platforms. This is accomplished through a two-phase commit process that ensures that data residing across multiple locations is properly synchronized.

- *High system availability*—Local autonomy ensures that local processing can continue even when a remote database is placed offline. Remote databases can be added to the distributed database management system without adversely affecting local processing.

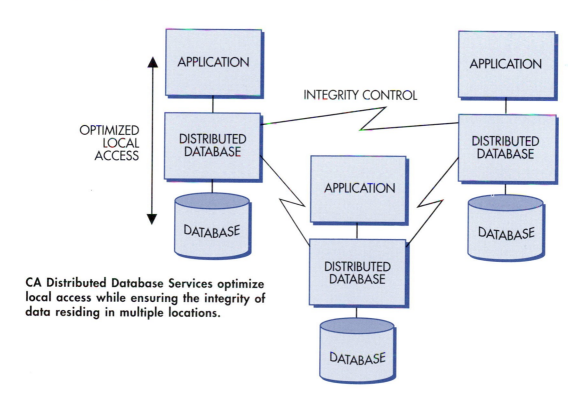

CA Distributed Database Services optimize local access while ensuring the integrity of data residing in multiple locations.

Distributed Database Implementation

CA Distributed Database Services currently provide the highest level of distributed database functionality in the industry. For example, no other vendor provides capabilities for the most sophisticated implementation of distributed database known as distributed request. CA Distributed Database Services fully support all four levels of distribution.

- *Remote request*—This level of distribution involves an application generating one or several units of work, each of which is limited to a single database call to a remote database. At this level, there is no transaction management across database operations.

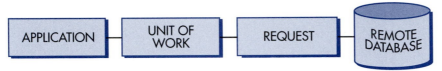

Remote request processing involves database requests to a single remote database.

- *Remote unit of work*—Within this level, an application invokes one or several units of work, each of which can make one or several database requests, all to the same remote database.

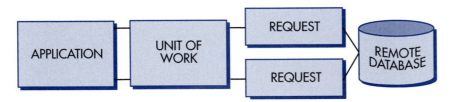

Remote unit of work support includes multiple requests to a single remote database.

- *Distributed unit of work*—Here, an application invokes one or several units of work, each of which spawns and manages multiple requests to remote databases. In turn, each request goes to a single database, but distributed database transaction management services bring together operations on several databases at several sites.

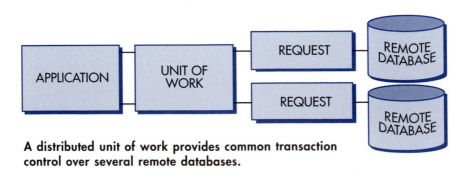

A distributed unit of work provides common transaction control over several remote databases.

• *Distributed request*—The most technically sophisticated level of distributed database support is distributed request. At this level, an application invokes units of work which, in turn, invoke one or several requests. Each request, however, is capable of spawning and managing multiple remote database operations.

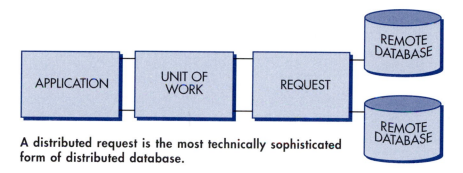

A distributed request is the most technically sophisticated form of distributed database.

Common Communication Interface

The existence of many different communications protocols on various platforms complicates efforts to provide a standard that allows software solutions to communicate with one another regardless of the location of the communicating functions or the communications software which connects various platforms.

IBM Systems Network Architecture (SNA) compatibility is one proposed standard. However, SNA compatibility is complicated by the existence of multiple protocols that meet SNA compatibility requirements. Furthermore, it is vendor specific and does not address multi-vendor environments. Given the current state of connectivity technology, all applications have been forced to deal with the specifics of the network software on each individual platform in order to communicate with another platform, especially another vendor platform. The development effort required to establish this connectivity is enormous and is always duplicated each time an additional application requires connectivity to another platform.

Even in single-vendor environments, lack of communications standards makes it difficult for solutions to communicate. Within IBM SNA, for example, there are several fundamentally different communications protocols that an application must understand in order to exchange data with its peers using network services. For example, the SNA LU6.2 protocol has been implemented in a number of different ways, requiring the sending application to understand which LU6.2 dialect a receiving application expects.

To resolve the difficulty of communicating across multiple platforms and to provide an effective standard, Computer Associates has developed the CA Common Communication Interface (CAICCI).

CAICCI surrounds communications and network software so that the enterprise solution can be insulated from the specifics of the environment. The enterprise solution communicates with CAICCI through a standard API. CAICCI then communicates the appropriate information to the targeted platform handling the specific communications requirements.

Even in traditional, centralized environments, CAICCI offers process-to-process communications facilities that standardize and simplify data interchanges between applications. Also, CAICCI provides the framework for future networked or distributed processing options as needed to support application or network growth.

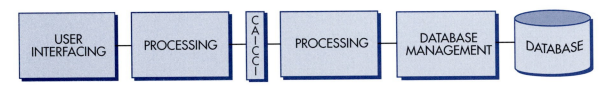

CAICCI promotes transparency, even in a traditional, centralized processing environment.

While CAICCI is used directly by several services of CA90s, it is crucial to the Distributed Processing Services. The functionality and insulation of the Distributed Processing Services from network requirements, made possible through the use of CAICCI, significantly simplifies the task of implementing cooperative processing, database server and distributed database capabilities in CA Enterprise Software Solutions.

CAICCI fully supports the various forms of cooperative and distributed information processing including peer-to-peer cooperative processing with the peer applications residing on either the same or different platforms; client-server configurations, allowing enterprise software to request a service from another application that may reside on another platform; database server and distributed database technology for communication across platforms and network transparency.

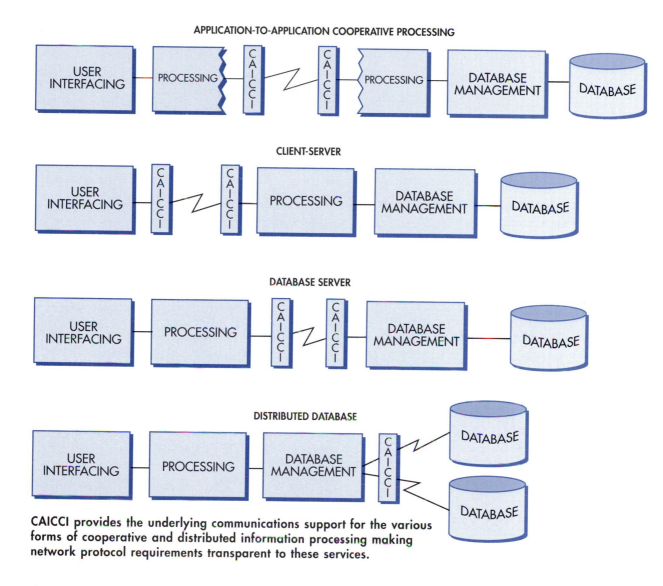

APPLICATION-TO-APPLICATION COOPERATIVE PROCESSING

CLIENT-SERVER

DATABASE SERVER

DISTRIBUTED DATABASE

CAICCI provides the underlying communications support for the various forms of cooperative and distributed information processing making network protocol requirements transparent to these services.

CAICCI Services

CAICCI provides a simplified communication interface that allows Enterprise Software Solutions to effectively manage communication across platforms. CAICCI provides the following services:

- *Program-To-Program (Peer-To-Peer) Communication*—Peer-to-peer communication provides programs at each end of a communications link that work as equal partners in managing the communication. Unlike many peer-to-peer communications protocols, CAICCI does not depend on the concept of primary/secondary applications. Regardless of the underlying communications media, CAICCI presents a true "full-duplex" view of the link, relieving applications from many session management tasks. If the physical link does not support true full-duplex communications, then CAICCI automatically handles all of the required link arbitration and queueing. More powerful applications can be designed using this service, than with traditionally used "terminal emulation" technology.

- *Application-To-Terminal Session*—CAICCI supports communication to a physical device rather than another application. Data being sent to the device may be edited so that the application need not be aware of any special device characteristics. Optionally, the application may construct complex terminal data streams and bypass CAICCI editing. Standard CAICCI network routing applies, so that communication to a physical device located across networks and platforms can occur.

- *Support For Synchronous And Asynchronous Processing Options*—Asychronous processing allows control to be returned to the application before the requested function is completed, thereby allowing the invoking program to proceed with other useful work while CAICCI performs the function. The synchronous processing option indicates that control should not be returned to the application until the requested function has been completed.

- *Transmission Management*—Data buffer transmissions are automatically handled by CAICCI, thus insulating applications from screen, key and timing dependencies. Additionally, CAICCI acts as a transmission manager, completely managing physical communications sessions between platforms. Applications can operate without regard for the direction of traffic, session or path management.

- *Optional Queueing Of Received Data*—Requests may be sent to an application that is busy performing other work or is otherwise unavailable. CAICCI will queue the data until the application is prepared to receive it. Additionally, this allows an application to retrieve arbitrarily lengthy data streams without needing to know ahead of time items such as buffer size.

- *Transparent Support For Physical Transmission Requirements*—CAICCI automatically handles different hardware requirements, character translation, data error detection and correction (when not handled by hardware), buffering, timing and management of internal sessions and conversations.

- *Parallel Conversations*—CAICCI multi-tasks conversations so that all products can use CAICCI services concurrently without experiencing delays or performance problems. Additionally, an individual application can talk to any number of applications concurrently.

- *Performance Optimization*—CAICCI optimizes data traffic based on response criteria and system load. Furthermore, it automatically performs load balancing across multiple links and handles data compression requirements. CAICCI will dynamically reconfigure the network load when bottlenecks occur.

- *Automatic Path Management*—CAICCI allows applications to exchange data with other applications that may reside on other platforms. In complex environments, the path between these applications may include many intermediate platforms with each using different communications protocols. CAICCI automatically selects the optimum path from source to target system, managing intermediate network transmissions as required.

- *Simplified Installation Requirements*—Since CAICCI handles communications services for all CA enterprise solutions, installation involves the definition of only one facility for each node. This provides a single point of control, a single set of network definitions and a single facility to monitor and tune.

- *Error Handling*—When CAICCI detects errors on a link, it will dynamically reconfigure to use an error-free link or, if necessary, it will dynamically add a link.

- *Built-In Diagnostic Aids*—Communications trace facilities are provided to simplify communications problem determination and resolution. Because CAICCI is a common tool employed by CA solutions, CAICCI provides superior and more thorough diagnostic capabilities than can be provided in any individual product, especially when problems occur due to the interaction of more than one product. These facilities enable many CA software solutions to be quickly and consistently supported in the event of any communications problem.

These CAICCI services are easily invoked using the simplified communication interface. The primary CAICCI functions and services are provided by verbs which are similar to traditional file I/O verbs such as: Open (open the file); Read (read from the file); Write (write to the file); and Close (close the file). The major verbs, corresponding to well-known universal communications functions, include *INITIALIZE* (or connect), *SEND*, *RECEIVE* and *TERMINATE*.

Unique extended functions are also provided by CAICCI. *CONVERSE* combines *SEND* and *RECEIVE* into a single function. *SPAWN* directs CAICCI to start a process (invoke a unit of work) within a specified network node. *STATUS* directs CAICCI to return a list of all receivers known to CAICCI. The list will consist of all local receiver IDs as well as any remote receivers (networked).

CAICCI also offers services that allow applications to exchange "structured" data, with type conversions and reformatting controlled by dictionary elements shipped with each data packet.

For example, if an application indicates that it requires "character" data, it may mean EBCDIC on IBM mainframes and ASCII elsewhere. By defining specific requirements in an external dictionary, the applications served by CAICCI can be assured of processing data in the format required without regard for type conversions.

Using the dictionary information, CAICCI can perform transparent type conversion, insulating applications from the need to know the detailed data requirements of their communications partners. (This structured information is defined in the data center information model included with CA Repository Services.)

Exchanging structured data can allow applications running on different platforms to be coded so as not to be sensitive to data representation.

Transparent Support For Environments

CAICCI makes use of the most effective protocols, to ensure efficient network management, as a means of communication within or across platforms. This process is totally transparent to the application. The application simply invokes CAICCI through a standard API. CAICCI also handles communications between applications on the same platform through cross-memory services.

CAICCI supports a wide range of communications and network software, insulating the requirements of these protocols from applications. Any of the operating systems supported by CAICCI can therefore communicate with each other.

CAICCI supports Local Area Networks (LANs) by themselves and in combination with gateways to midrange and mainframe systems. This allows the implementation of both application-to-application and client-server configurations over the LAN, with PC applications talking to PC applications, with PC applications talking to midrange or mainframe applications, and with PC clients talking to PC, midrange, or mainframe servers. CAICCI uniquely enables different combinations of LAN, SNA and DECnet networks to be used together.

The architecture of CAICCI allows it to be easily extended to address new requirements. Additional platforms and communications protocols can be supported by CAICCI without affecting the software solutions.

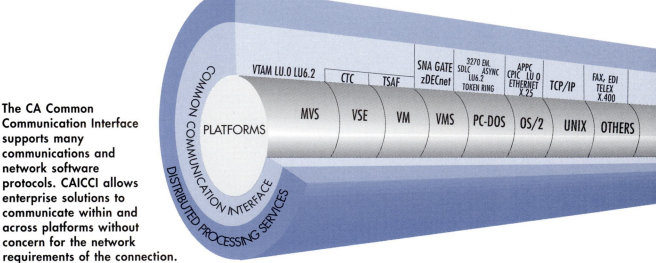

The CA Common Communication Interface supports many communications and network software protocols. CAICCI allows enterprise solutions to communicate within and across platforms without concern for the network requirements of the connection.

Security And Integrity Of Data

CAICCI includes comprehensive security interfaces to ensure that all data routed across a network reaches the destination in a secure manner. CAICCI uses the CA Standard Security Facility (CAISSF) in order to perform resource checks for all application requests. In cases where physical devices are involved (such as an application-to-terminal session), CAICCI will have the option to authenticate the terminal user via a signon facility. The CAICCI *SPAWN* facility, which executes units of work across network nodes, will guarantee that the *SPAWN* entity inherits the security environment of the user that initiated it. Data packets shipped across a network are verified using a combination of message authentication codes and encryption. Classification labels may be supplied to CAICCI and will be used in the authentication process. Various client controls are available to control the level and type of security checking and authentication to be performed.

Open Architecture For Client Application Integration

If clients follow standard protocols, CAICCI will accept user-written sessions and will deal with them appropriately. CAICCI can interface with native networking software in such a way as to support popular communications facilities that do not conform to the CAICCI API.

As an example, client applications running on IBM platforms will be able to use CICS (GDS) LU6.2 commands to communicate with CAICCI-based applications.

Summary

The Distributed Processing Services of CA90s provide full support for the various configurations of cooperative processing, database server and distributed database technologies. Advanced communications capabilities ensure simplified, streamlined sharing of distributed information and processing across multi-vendor, multi-operating system networked environments. In addition, the Distributed Processing Services provide CA clients with the freedom to choose the computing platform sized to the task.

Through these services, enterprises can take maximum advantage of the tremendous benefits that distributed processing across multiple platforms offers, while remaining confident that the integrity of corporate information is assured. The ability to implement distributed processing across the enterprise ensures the most efficient use of the variety of available hardware platforms, particularly the underutilized power found on desktop systems.

In addition, the ability to distribute information and processing for more effective, local decision making, positions enterprises to compete more effectively in global markets.

While the Service Layers provide important functions utilized by the Enterprise Software Solutions, it is the solutions themselves that provide the functionality required by the enterprise. Computer Associates provides an extensive array of integrated software solutions that address virtually every aspect of enterprise computing and position information systems professionals to meet today's challenges. The benefits derived from CA90s and its guiding principles are multiplied by the breadth of Enterprise Software Solutions that incorporate them.

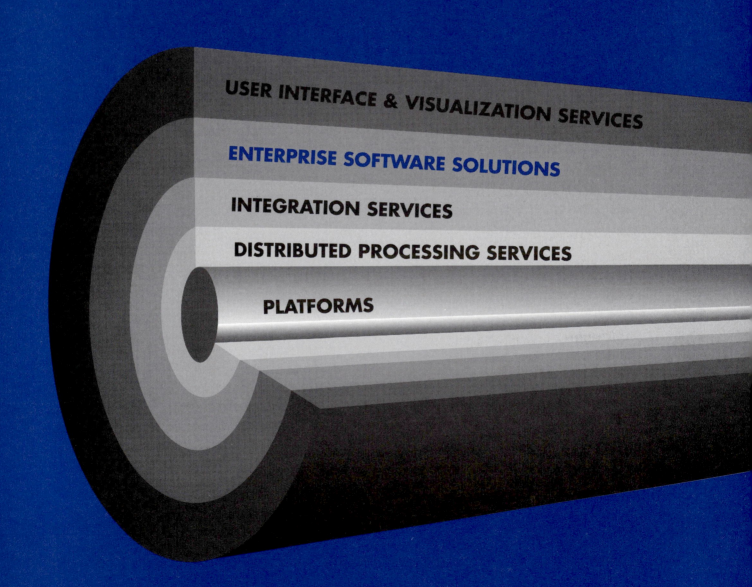

USER INTERFACE & VISUALIZATION SERVICES

ENTERPRISE SOFTWARE SOLUTIONS

INTEGRATION SERVICES

DISTRIBUTED PROCESSING SERVICES

PLATFORMS

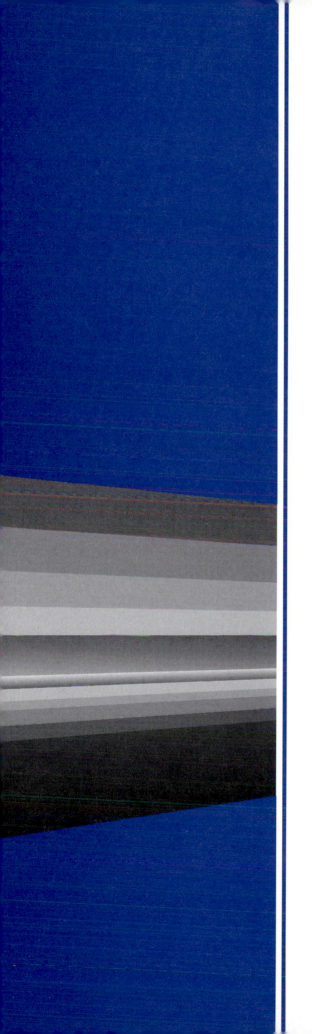

SECTION III

The Enterprise Software Solutions

CHAPTER

Systems Management
Software

The Systems Management Software Challenges

Evolving beyond basic applications such as billing and inventory, information systems are now used universally to support critical business decisions, to directly support customers and to support the manufacturing process. Behind these sophisticated business information systems remains the need to manage and maintain the diverse and often incompatible operating systems and hardware environments needed for their execution. Due to the significant contribution of information systems to the effectiveness of the enterprise as a whole, the management and control of computer resources now directly affects the competitive performance of the enterprise. The ability of IS to establish and meet required levels of performance, reliability and availability, while staying within budgetary constraints, is the measure of its success or failure to support the enterprise.

However, information systems professionals face daunting challenges in the 90s as they work to manage and control complex networks and data centers. These major challenges involve establishing and consistently meeting service-level agreements with end users, controlling costs to meet service levels at the lowest possible level of investment, and protecting the wealth of enterprise information and key resources that often span multiple operating systems and hardware platforms, while ensuring complete system integrity.

The traditional mainframe view of information management is being rapidly replaced by a more global view, including distributed processing, downsizing and decentralizing of processing resources. Networking together vast collections of diverse and complementary information processing technologies are required to address all of the needs of the enterprise. Within this view, systems management must recognize that although midrange and micro computing environments have been traditionally left to their own devices, when combined in networked configurations these machines collectively represent a significant investment in information processing power, and have the same needs for automation, resource management, security and data integrity that have evolved into the standard Systems Management functionality we know today on large mainframe systems.

The advent of open systems, and the promise of interchangeability of hardware for processing in UNIX-based environments, advances a new challenge, the challenge of how information management will ensure that the same level of integrity, quality, reliability, and cost controls that their mainframes provided can be achieved in this new heterogeneous processing environment. It is through the Systems Management Software, provided within the CA90s Enterprise Software Solution layer, that CA has answered this vital need for the next decade.

Service-Level Management And Cost Control

Service-level management defines the process of identifying, documenting, measuring and accounting for system use and performance against requirements agreed upon with end users of the systems' services. Service-level agreements are expressed in terms that relate to end users' business requirements such as system response time, production turn-around time, report delivery time, responsiveness to problems or computer availability. Effective service-level management reduces the incidence and severity of errors, detects them promptly and enables the system to recover from them quickly. The result is improved system reliability, availability and serviceability (RAS), increased throughput and greater system functionality.

Efficient and effective systems management, operating under budgetary constraints, requires that service-level commitments be met at the lowest possible level of investment. All information processing resources need to be analyzed, managed and controlled, including staff, hardware, software, network and data resources, in order to minimize costs.

Data center automation is the only way to provide optimum service levels at minimum cost. While advances in technology have resulted in faster, more powerful computers, IS organizations are still plagued by an extraordinary number of tasks requiring continual manual intervention.

Data center automation is even more critical in light of today's complex multi-platform, multi-vendor environments. The complexity of these environments, often characterized by incompatible systems as well as redundancy of data and functions, places huge demands on the training and cross-training of data center staff, at a time when qualified personnel are growing increasingly scarce.

Cross-platform resource accounting and comprehensive network inventory management solutions that allow change to be managed, problems to be tracked and serviced, and costs to be appropriately identified and allocated are essential to gain and keep control over these complex environments. A direct connection between accounting capabilities and data center automation software also ensures that resources applied to automated capabilities are properly recorded, the benefits of data center automation accurately measured and the system effectively tuned to best meet business needs.

The requirements described above can only be met by Systems Management Software which, largely characterized by its rule-based, policy-oriented nature, is well-suited to automating the detailed operational tasks involved in running the enterprise network. Utilizing comprehensive and totally integrated software solutions, as well as simplifying the training required to use them enables personnel to devote more time to analysis and management. The results are substantial gains in productivity and system reliability as well as decreased costs.

Security Control

The growth in networked departmental computers and desktop systems, along with the diversity of available hardware and software solutions have also complicated efforts to ensure system integrity and protect data and key resources against loss, damage or misuse. While security requirements are in large part determined by the specific needs of the systems applications they service, consistent access control services across applications, platforms and network dimensions are essential.

CA Systems Management Software Meets These Challenges

CA Systems Management Software delivers integrated, total data center automation capabilities that enable IS management to provide the consistent, high service levels required by the enterprise while effectively controlling costs and ensuring protection of valuable data and resources.

CA90s provides cross-platform integration and coordination of Systems Management Software that, for the first time, enables truly cost-effective management of all components of the enterprise-wide information processing systems: IBM mainframes under MVS, VSE and VM, Digital VAX Systems, UNIX Systems, Tandem Guardian Systems and (beginning with access control) PC-DOS systems.

The rule-based policies that govern data center procedures are particularly well suited to automation and can be handled quickly and accurately by Systems Management Software without the need for specialized programs. This automation capability is essential in addressing the complex activities of multi-vendor, multi-operating system networked environments where a variety of procedures are generally followed due to the variation in capabilities provided by the native platforms. CA Systems Management Software simplifies the management of these complex environments by extending native platform capabilities wherever necessary to ensure operational consistency regardless of platform.

The otherwise numerous and complex procedures are significantly reduced, enabling operations staff to become familiar with all aspects of a streamlined, unified system. This dramatically reduces the training required of operational staff, particularly in complicated subsystem procedures, and eliminates the need for multiple subsystem specialists to closely monitor data center and network activities.

Through the Service Layers of CA90s, CA Systems Management Software also provides advanced computer-based realtime training, interactive assistance and documentation look-up capabilities to further reduce training costs and increase staff productivity.

The CA Systems Management Software solutions extend far beyond the basic services provided by native operating systems to cover the broad range of interrelated functions required to manage and control data center and network activity. In addition, they utilize the CA90s Service Layers to interact with each other, adding value to the enterprise's information systems as a whole. CA90s therefore describes a much broader view of Systems Management Software than that defined by any other architecture. But this approach, where all components work together across multiple platforms is essential to maintaining sufficient responsiveness to the continually evolving priorities of business-driven information processing requirements.

Automating each area of systems management does not in itself result in a complete and successful approach to systems management. Each component of the systems management solution must support and communicate with every other component in order to achieve total data center automation. For example, enterprise-wide information security cannot be ensured if each systems management solution uses its own security tables. Problem and change management cannot keep pace with the dynamic activities of large and complex environments if software that addresses functions such as scheduling, report distribution, storage management and security cannot open and update problem incidents automatically. Clearly, global work load management is unattainable unless each platform provides a work load scheduling and resource balancing capability that interfaces with all other platforms.

It is this essential, yet unprecedented high level of systems integration that sets the CA90s image of Systems Management apart from others. Complete and effective integration requires both a design for integration and an architecture that supports development and enhancement of the completely integrated solution. CA90s, through the Integration Services Layer, provides the tools and architecture needed to implement complete and integrated systems management.

It is nearly impossible, and economically inadvisable, especially in multi-platform environments, for an enterprise to depend on its internal staff for the integration of disparate components obtained from numerous sources in order to achieve enterprise-wide systems management. CA's multi-platform, integrated solutions enable enterprises to achieve integrated Systems Management without requiring the substantial investment of time, money and effort required for the in-house development and extensive customization that accompanies disparate, non-integrated solutions.

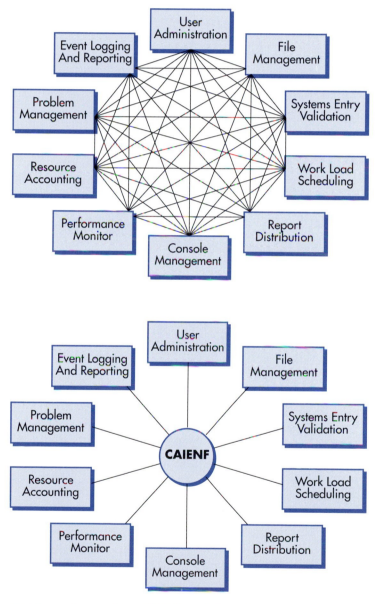

CA90s services, such as CAIENF, enable the integration of systems management functions without an uncontrollable and unmanageable explosion of interfaces.

CA Systems Management Software provides a fully integrated solution that covers the areas of: Automated Production Control; Automated Storage Management; Performance Management and Accounting; Data Center Administration; and Security, Control and Audit.

To completely automate the data center and derive maximum benefit, all of these components must be present. Vendors who offer only a part of this functionality and limit the functionality to specific platforms, cannot effectively assist IS management in meeting their service-level objectives.

For management of UNIX systems, mainframes and mixed networks, the CA enterprise-wide systems management approach also includes a System Manager's Workstation based on a UNIX desktop system. Using a graphical user interface operating under Motif, the System Manager's Workstation presents a unified view of all of the CA Systems Management solutions on local as well as remote systems.

The CA Systems Management solutions cover the broad range of functions required to manage and control data center and network activity and to provide complete and effective data center automation.

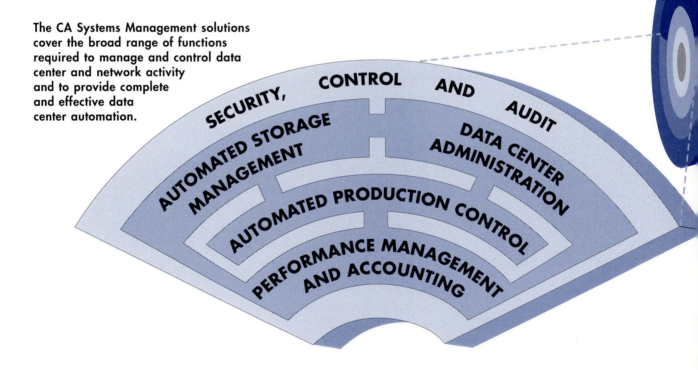

Automated Production Control

Computer Associates provides the most comprehensive and integrated set of solutions for Automated Production Control. These solutions cover all areas of functionality including:

Work Load Management—complete automated management of production work loads including work load balancing, automatic submission and tracking of work based on user-defined scheduling criteria, priority and system resource availability. This ensures that work is completed correctly and that critical deadlines are met.

Rerun, Restart and Recovery—automates the often complex, manual-intensive and error-prone rerun and recovery process, enabling processing to restart at the optimum recovery point. In addition, it automatically handles the otherwise time-consuming manual procedures such as job setup, data set recovery and backout.

Console Management—improves operating efficiency and reduces errors by automating the handling of console messages. It provides an advanced message/action capability that can alter, suppress or reply to messages or initiate other actions, such as automatically issuing IPL/IMLs, alerts (through voice and pager notification capabilities), commands, or invoking programs based on the content, frequency and other characteristics of the message traffic. In addition, selective action based on specific console and terminal IDs allows the assignment of consoles to specialized applications, such as network monitoring, system monitoring or tape mount processing. A simulation capability is also provided to assist in the development and verification of these event/action criteria.

When used in conjunction with a programmable workstation, this software provides a single focal point for all console operation activities in a multi-CPU, multi-operating system, network environment. In addition, remote access to perform console management is available through remote dial-ups (PC, remote TSO, CICS, Session) or through the telephone using the latest voice and touch-tone technology.

Report Distribution—provides extensive capabilities for the flexible and efficient production, tracking and distribution of reports. This results in speeding the delivery time, increasing the accuracy and improving the tracking of reports. Facilities are provided that automatically identify pages from existing reports, place them into bundles, and sort them by delivery location prior to actual printing. These capabilities provide end users with the information they want, when and where they need it, while reducing or eliminating redundant information and the materials and efforts that are wasted in its distribution.

Automated report distribution software also provides online viewing capabilities that can reduce the need for hard copy of reports as well as the option to select all or parts of reports for printing. Report archiving capabilities enable the storing of reports offline for auditing purposes and for future viewing or reprinting.

CA Report Management software on intelligent workstations extends report management capabilities by enabling end users to receive reports as files on their local computer. The ability to merge, annotate or change reports using a familiar computer is automated by the workstation-based software, and redistribution of these new reports is provided through interaction with the software on the host system.

Control Language Validation—virtually all systems in use today provide an interpretive control language for defining the execution of batch and online processing. Examples of these languages include IBM's Job Control Language or JCL, Digital's VMS Digital Control Language (DCL), and the UNIX Shell Script language. CA's design for systems management includes complete, advanced control language validation capabilities that reduce or eliminate errors that can cause failures during production execution, and that aid the end user in diagnosing problems with control language programs. In addition, this software enforces site-specific JCL standards while providing the reports and cross-reference information that are needed for future maintenance.

Report Balancing—extensive, automated report and file balancing capabilities that enable a quality level to be achieved that is unavailable through manual efforts. In addition to automatically ensuring the accuracy of reports after they are printed, this software can uniquely catch errors during the execution of production work cycles, both enabling fast and accurate resolution of problems, and preventing the completion of in-error production runs and the distribution of incorrect report output.

Production Documentation—complete and consistent centralized online documentation system for the production control environment. Integration with other production control software enables documentation efforts to be automated and centralized, ensuring accessible and accurate information essential to data center operations, and particularly for contingency planning, disaster recovery and future maintenance.

Automated Storage Management

Automated Storage Management software significantly extends the native operating system's capabilities of storage and resource management. This software optimizes performance and access to information, ensuring availability, integrity and reliability regardless of the various media device types and differing configurations of mainframes, midrange computers, PCs and LANs that define the information processing environment.

Multimedia Management—uses a rule-based, policy-oriented design to provide comprehensive storage resource functions for a wide variety of media, both permanently mounted file storage devices and removable tape, WORM, and erasable optical technologies. These functions include space management, allocation control and management, I/O optimization, volume defragmentation and mount management. Each of these capabilities is designed to provide the best possible utilization of the storage devices available while maintaining the service levels defined by the enterprise's storage management policies.

Extended Data Management—enhances and fully automates all data management functions regardless of platform, including reformatting, sorting, compression and optimization of data seamlessly and independent of physical file organization and data format. In addition, it provides facilities for archiving, backup, movement, reorganization and other maintenance functions critical to efficiently managing the storage environment.

Performance and Error Management—through data integrity and device failure recovery facilities, system throughput can be optimized and disruptions caused by failures can be minimized. In addition, high-cost, high-performance options of disk devices can be exploited to their full potential.

Security, Control And Audit

Securing of information resources, wherever they are held, is critical to protecting the organization's information assets. Typically, these resources are now distributed across heterogeneous platforms including large-scale MVS central systems, departmental VAX/VMS nodes, LANs and individual user PC workstations. CA security solutions, engineered using CA90s services, provide a unique level of protection across these diverse operating environments and heterogeneous platforms.

Security and Access Control—provides effective asset protection including identification and registration of users across networks, control of unauthorized access to resources and virus detection and prevention. In addition, through simplified single-point signon capabilities and network-level security, users need only to identify themselves once, by supplying their user ID and password, when they establish their first network session.

In addition to securing those resources typically managed by the operating system, such as files, libraries and programs, the CA access control facilities are utilized by all CA Enterprise Software Solutions for securing their internal processing. This enables the enterprise to have centralized control over critical functions that are not native to the operating system, such as the ability to define or execute production schedules, the ability to define report bundles and designate recipients, and the ability to issue critical console commands. Integration with business solutions and information management solutions enables centralized control of critical business information, such as billing and client information, and control of specific views of mission critical information within databases.

Audit—provides automatic audit and integrity checking, monitors violations, identifies security exposures and validates product installations

Performance Management And Accounting

CA Performance Management and Accounting software provides the broadest spectrum of integrated, sophisticated software solutions to manage performance, accounting and future planning for the operating systems, networks and subsystems, and file management systems as well as for Database Management Systems such as CA-DATACOM/DB, CA-IDMS/DB, CA-DB/UNIX and CA-DB/VAX.

Performance Management—optimizes system performance by providing realtime monitoring of hardware and software, historical reporting, expert system performance analysis and automatic tuning recommendations.

Resource Accounting—helps control and account for costs by providing resource utilization measurement facilities, chargeback capabilities for all data processing resources and services, and management level reporting on resource consumption broken down by such organizational groupings as user, department and cost center. Resource accounting is a key element in service level management, as it provides both information systems management and the end-user community with a window into how computer resources are being used, and where within the organization these resources are being consumed. CA resource accounting solutions help the enterprise move accountability for the purchase and allocation of computer resources closer to the end user. By providing a breakdown of where and how money is spent, these solutions enable the enterprise to better control costs and to simplify the process of justifying expenses.

Capacity Planning—enables planning for future computing needs by analyzing current utilization levels, assessing the impact of growth rates on service levels and forecasting future system requirements using expert system technology.

Data Center Administration

Computer Associates provides an integrated Data Center Administration system based on data dictionary services that easily evolve toward the use of CA Repository Services. This system enables the effective management of enterprise-wide hardware and software inventories and assets including mainframes and all the communications equipment and links, and all the end-point terminals and workstations. With integrated incident tracking, change administration, financial analysis and configuration management, enterprises can manage resources effectively across multiple hardware environments.

Problem/Change Management—provides incident tracking and change coordination

Inventory Configuration—allows hardware and software configuration placement

Financial Analysis—provides order tracking, vendor contract maintenance and invoice replication capabilities

Customization Facility—allows end-user tailoring of screens and reports

Network inventory management provides the means to track system assets as they move and as they are upgraded or changed. Both the hardware and software configurations are recorded. This extensive collecting of configuration information, combined with the capabilities of CA90s database/repository services, enables the integrated management of data center administration. For example, system asset management data can now be combined with resource utilization data from Performance Management and Accounting Software, to allow cost recovery and effective IS enterprise-wide financial management.

Configuration data is also used to support change management. Impact analysis, change approval and change process initiation and tracking are now easily achievable due to the database/repository foundation.

In addition, network service management supports the tracking of service incidents or problems and provides the means to manage the resolution process and to track resolution performance.

System Manager's Workstation

The Systems Management solutions may be administered from an integrated GUI-based user interface operating under the Motif environment—the "System Manager's Workstation." Operating on a UNIX desktop system or graphical terminal, this workstation may be used to administer a single UNIX system, a network of like or unlike UNIX systems, a remote IBM mainframe or even a heterogeneous network containing mainframes and like or unlike UNIX systems.

System Manager's Workstation provides systems management for a homogeneous or heterogeneous network.

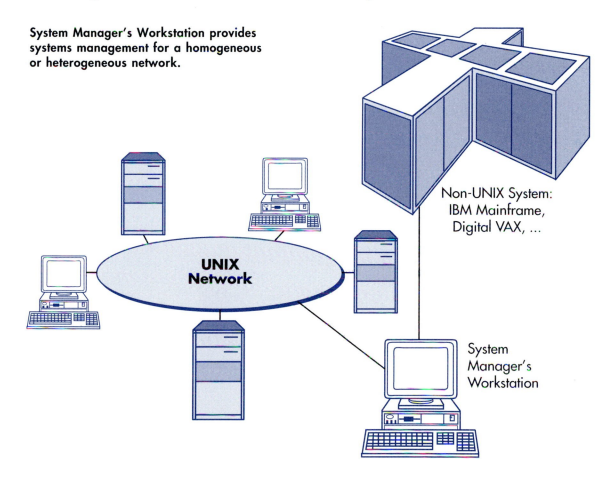

Non-UNIX System:
IBM Mainframe,
Digital VAX, ...

UNIX Network

System Manager's Workstation

Through the graphical user interface, the System Manager's Workstation provides an easily understood window into the world of systems management. This modern interface reduces the complexity of systems management and gives an intuitive and logical view of otherwise complex issues. Operating under Motif, which is based on the X Windows System, the System Manager's Workstation can, of course, operate on a lower cost X-terminal as well as a full-fledged workstation.

The CA Systems Management solution also utilizes the power of the intelligent workstation to assist in the analysis and decision making processes of systems management through simulation, modeling and expert system technologies.

CA90s And Systems Management Software

All of the specialized Systems Management Software solutions are closely tied together. Through integration, a complete, enterprise-wide automated data center can be created with the benefits of the combined solutions far exceeding the sum of the individual products.

CA90s enables CA to deliver Systems Management Solutions that perform better, are more deeply integrated, exhibit greater reliability and are consistent and interoperable across hardware platforms. These benefits enable clients to make significant strides in achieving total data center automation, in meeting service-level requirements, and in controlling costs while maximizing the return on investment.

The layered architecture of CA90s enables Systems Management Software solutions to take advantage of the common set of engineering precepts, above and beyond the features and functions applied to solving a discrete problem. These universal capabilities of Systems Management Software reside in the Service Layers. While not all services are available to all Systems Management Software solutions today across all operating systems and hardware platforms, each of the technologies found in the Service Layers already exist in many CA solutions. Computer Associates is committed to extending the utilization of these services as needed by clients. Examples of the usefulness of CA90s Service Layers to Systems Management Software, both in the future and available today, are numerous.

Multi-Platform Capabilities

The first step in addressing the systems management needs of any enterprise is to have equivalent solutions that run on all platforms used by that enterprise, and that communicate with one another, allowing for a common method of accessing and employing these solutions.

Computer Associates Systems Management Software includes support for the systems used by our clients today and, through CA90s, enables rapid and efficient extension of those solutions to the platforms they will be using tomorrow.

The security area is a good example of the cross-platform capabilities of CA90s. Security administration in multiple platform environments is a difficult task of enormous importance for every enterprise. Recent well-publicized events have shown the danger of unauthorized access and its tremendous potential for damage. What is less well recognized is that access control is as much a problem of administration as of technology. "The hackers don't break codes, they look for open doors." Passwords and access privileges are often not maintained properly across the multitude of systems. Different systems have different levels of access control, ranging from very strong to weak or nonexistent, with completely different methods of administration. The problem, for example, of removing all authorizations of a departed employee, across all systems, some of which are remote, using different administration methods, is a daunting one.

By relying on the service layers of CA90s, the CA security solution provides consistent protection across IBM MVS, VSE and VM, Digital VAX/VMS, Tandem Guardian, as well as several UNIX and PC-DOS environments. CA-ACF2 and CA-TOP SECRET use the Event Notification Facility (CAIENF) for integration with each operating system as required and the Common Communication Interface (CAICCI) for communication between different systems, in order to integrate the security systems on each platform. Where appropriate, this integration incorporates security systems native to the platform. The benefits of common administration accrue regardless of the access control technology.

No hardware vendor nor any other software vendor is able to offer a security solution that operates across the multiplicity of hardware platforms commonly present in an enterprise's computing environment. The level of protection afforded by CA security solutions operating within the CA90s software architecture is unrivaled in the marketplace today.

Through this extensive functionality and through the CA Standard Security Facility (CAISSF) described in the chapter on Integration Services, Computer Associates has already set the commercial security standard for the industry.

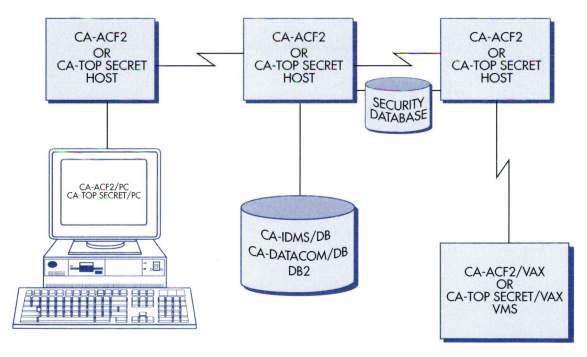

Consistent security protection is available across MVS, VSE, VM, Digital VMS and IBM PC-DOS environments through the use of common communications services and the extensive capabilities of CA-ACF2 and CA-TOP SECRET.

User Interface And Visualization Services

Interaction with the user has been a traditional weak point of systems management products. While business applications have always concentrated on the presentation of data, systems products have always addressed first the need to communicate with and control the operating system. Through the use of User Interface and Visualization Services, CA Systems Management Software can address this weakness.

CA Systems Management Software is provided with a common "look and feel" based on modern user interfaces.

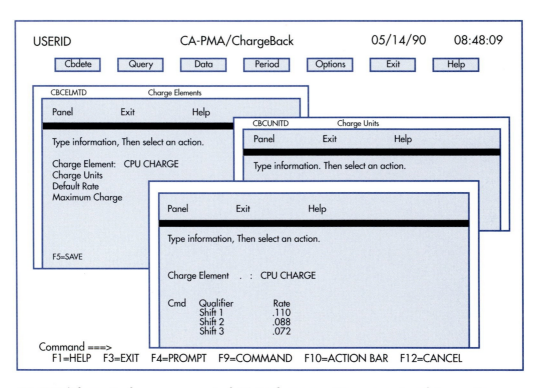

CA-PMA/ChargeBack, a component of CA Performance Management and Accounting solutions, provides a common "look and feel" based on a modern user interface that follows IBM CUA guidelines.

Within each platform, a common interface is maintained that is both appropriate to the platform and familiar to the user. For example, CA supports the IBM SAA CUA user interface standard on IBM platforms while also embracing the similar Motif windowed look for Digital and Hewlett–Packard UNIX systems. A consistent operation and terminology is provided regardless of platform, enabling the user of CA systems management solutions to leverage expertise in the operation of a CA solution when moving from one platform to another. Maintaining consistency in operation and navigation of the user interface also enables fast and intuitive definition of systems management policies that include resources and rules for several platforms.

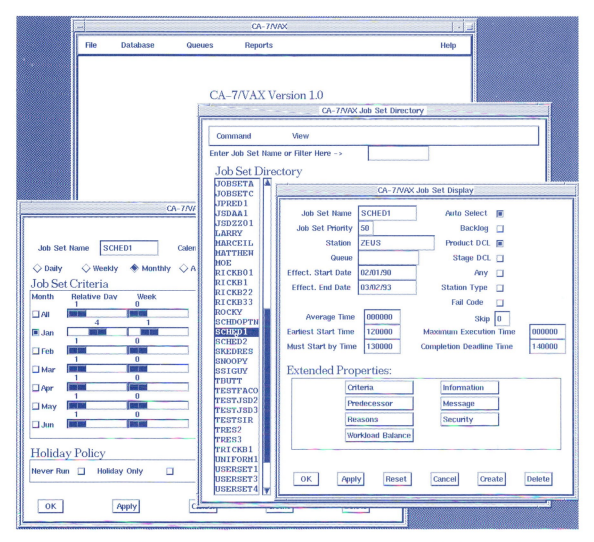

CA-7, running on VAX and UNIX workstations, presents a graphical user interface based on Motif.

The User Interface and Visualization Services of CA90s enable the use of these modern windowed interfaces, not only on intelligent workstations and X-terminal devices, but also on predominantly terminal-based systems such as IBM mainframes.

In addition, these Visualization services offer the use of new technologies, such as voice and computer-based training and online assistance, to significantly improve the productivity of IS staff.

Voice Services are employed in systems software to support unattended operations, remote problem notification, and to improve interaction between the system and those responsible for monitoring and maintaining the operation of the system. Voice Services extend the ability of staff members to rapidly address problems and unusual situations and play a key role in ensuring that high service levels are met and maintained.

For example, phone paging for problem notification and response is a key feature of CA-OPERA/PC, which can establish a broad range of policies to direct paging and notification of responsible individuals for problem solving. Voice can also be used to include announcement of messages, allowing operators to be notified immediately of required intervention without needing to constantly monitor the console; generation of messages for storage on phone queues, to allow access to accumulated information about problems, or current status, to be accessed remotely via any phone line; and voice response actions, allowing the remote user to respond to problems through the phone keypad with voice verification of the requested action.

Advanced computer-aided training, through the Online Consultant, is one of the unique capabilities offered across the CA Systems Management Software line. It integrates tutorials, online documentation, voice and video training while interacting with a realtime application. This technology is already providing multimedia help and assistance for users of CA-7, a work load scheduling system. The CA-7/OLC uses context-driven expert systems technology to monitor user interactions with the system. When a problem occurs, or on request, the CA-7/OLC is able to retrieve text, graphics and audio from high-capacity video disk storage to help resolve problems or provide instruction and assistance.

All of the services provided by the User Interface and Visualization Services are effective in reducing the time between problem occurrence and resolution. The right personnel are always accessible and are provided with the needed information quickly and easily to minimize resolution time.

Integration Services

CA90s Integration Services significantly simplify the interaction between individual solutions and between solutions and the underlying platforms. These services, including event notification, database, repository, and security; represent a natural progression of the efforts CA has expended over the years in integrating the current product lines and in consistently blending newly developed and acquired technologies with those already in place.

The CA Event Notification Facility (CAIENF) is a key element in the integration of Systems Management Software. It provides a number of unique opportunities and capabilities for systems products that are not available from any other vendor. While other vendors offer operating system independence, enabling an application written in a high-level language to be carried over intact to several diverse operating systems, these applications do not perform or manage any part of the operating system interface itself. No hardware vendor is working to standardize the method for interacting with the operating system and no hardware vendor offers systems management software that is identical across multiple operating systems.

CA-SCHEDULER, a component of CA Automated Production Control solutions, uses CAIENF to retrieve specific operating system event information and to provide recovery information from the CAIENF database.

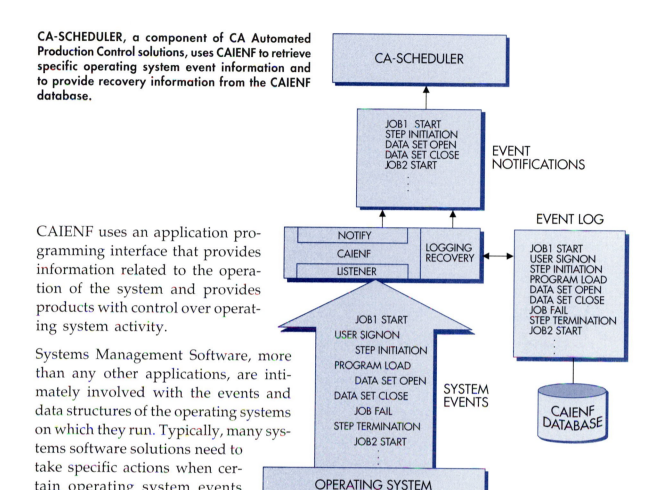

CAIENF uses an application programming interface that provides information related to the operation of the system and provides products with control over operating system activity.

Systems Management Software, more than any other applications, are intimately involved with the events and data structures of the operating systems on which they run. Typically, many systems software solutions need to take specific actions when certain operating system events occur.

An example is when an output data set is created by a user application. The tape management system must track the existence of the new file and perhaps note that a previous file generation is now no longer required under the retention rules established for that data set. The work load scheduling system may be able to start a job that needs this data set as input. The security system must authorize that the data set can be created by a certain user. Job accounting will record chargeback data about the file and volume ownership.

CAIENF provides a single point of recognition that an event such as a file close has occurred. All products interested in that event pre-register their interest and are then notified when the event occurs. Through the use of a data dictionary, each product is provided with only those data items of interest concerning the event. Through the data dictionary, data items are formatted to meet the requirements of each application.

The use of CAIENF also provides insulation from changes in the data structures and the processing of the underlying operating systems and from the differences between operating systems across the enterprise network. These changes can be handled easily and quickly by CAIENF rather than requiring it to be handled separately in each application. For example, when IBM announced MVS/ESA and, later, VSE/ESA, CA was able to make the required changes, once, through the Event Notification Facility. This enabled CA to make Systems Management Software not only compatible with ESA, but it also enabled the software to take advantage of ESA's full capabilities. All this was remarkably accomplished by the time IBM made ESA generally available to IBM clients.

The Event Notification Facility is an evolution of technology developed by CA over a number of years. It represents a proven approach that is now in use in CA client sites all over the world.

Database Management Services

Traditionally, systems products used specialized file structures or access methods that addressed the specific needs of the product, but which were limited by their inability to share information with other products. Through the Integration Services layer of CA90s, CA Systems Management Software can take advantage of the data sharing capabilities of database management systems, including advanced relational database support, without sacrificing performance.

The dedication of database services to the optimization and support of advanced file access provides Systems Management Software with the flexibility to address, for example, the complex reporting needs of today's heterogeneous environments. The ability to relate and report across product and platform boundaries enables Information Systems managers to join all aspects of the information processing environment into a single, cohesive reporting set.

For example, CA-PMA/ChargeBack, a comprehensive chargeback, inventory and capacity planning system, utilizes the CA90s database services to combine data from CA solutions and other data sources. By combining the power of the CA database engines with the wealth of data accumulated through all of the CA solutions in use, CA-PMA/ChargeBack provides the most comprehensive set of tools available today for evaluating and reporting on service levels.

CA-NETMAN, a component of CA Data Center Administration solutions, utilizes relational database technology to enable users to view and manipulate problem, change, inventory and financial management information as needed through ad hoc query and reporting capabilities.

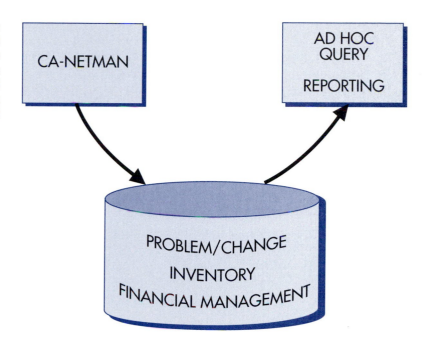

Data Center Administration software provides another good example of the use of database technology in Systems Management Software. The integrated functions of CA's Data Center Administration software utilize relational database technology to enable users to view and manipulate problem, change, inventory and financial management information as needed through ad hoc query and reporting capabilities.

Another major benefit of the database services are the provisions for backup and recovery. Journaling and forward recovery are a standard part of database integrity features, and when used in combination with systems products, provide a much needed answer to the traditional problem of file recovery following system outages or product outages.

The application of standardized database services to systems management products also simplifies and accelerates the migration of solutions to additional platforms. CA-PMA/ChargeBack is again a good example. CA-PMA/ChargeBack uses the SQL-capable, portable database interface of the CA90s Integration Services. Since SQL has become a standard on many of the platforms in use today, CA-PMA/ChargeBack was able to be moved with no change to the underlying technology from the IBM MVS mainframe environment to the Digital VAX/VMS environment and can be used with very little change on UNIX platforms as well. These new platform capabilities were achieved only a few months after the basic mainframe version of CA-PMA/ChargeBack was available, clearly demonstrating the advantages of developing products with common services and common standards.

Distributed Processing Services

Systems Management Software needs to be flexible enough to match the modes of operation required by the enterprise. In some enterprises, centralized systems management will be required. In others, decentralized operations with some centralized consolidation and control will be appropriate.

An example of the ways that CA90s enables CA to deliver solutions that can operate in either centralized or decentralized organizations can be given in the area of work load management. In a centralized network, a large-scale IBM MVS host may be surrounded by a number of distributed smaller nodes, perhaps Digital VAXclusters. The distributed nodes may be unattended, controlled and maintained from the central host with no data processing-trained staff present.

All work load schedules can be maintained at the central host and automatically distributed and executed as required to the outlying nodes. Common communications services would provide system interconnection. The progress and monitoring of processing on all nodes is accomplished through the Event Notification Facility. From an application perspective on the central host, the complexities of the different environments and the network distribution are effectively masked. Processing events that occur on the distributed VAXcluster nodes are the same from an application perspective as if the events occur locally.

The benefit to the user is that all the differences between these operating environments are masked. No data processing specialists are required at the remote sites. Operations staff at the central system can effectively and, in large part, automatically manage the entire network.

Alternately, peer-to-peer networks exist where work load management involves some level of coordinated processing between largely independent systems. Departmental systems that are mostly independent but have some consolidation and summarization requirements would be an example.

In this environment, work load scheduling is accomplished separately on each system with a relatively infrequent need for coordinated, dependent schedules across systems. This might be for end-of-period reporting, for instance. For these cases, ways of making processing schedules on one system dependent on processing events on another system on a peer-to-peer basis are required. Through the use of CA90s services, these requirements are being met by enterprises using CA solutions today.

CA-OPERA and CA-OPERA/PC are good examples of the distributed processing capabilities available with CA90s. The cooperative processing between these mainframe and remote console management systems allows the notification of critical events that occur on the mainframe to a PC workstation via a remote pager. This ensures immediate responsiveness to any recovery situation. The cooperative processing capability is further extended to allow remote IPL/IML of the mainframe system in the event of an operating system failure.

Another example of the effective use of distributed processing is CA tape management solutions, components of CA Automated Storage Management, that synchronize and control tape management functions across MVS, VSE and VM platforms.

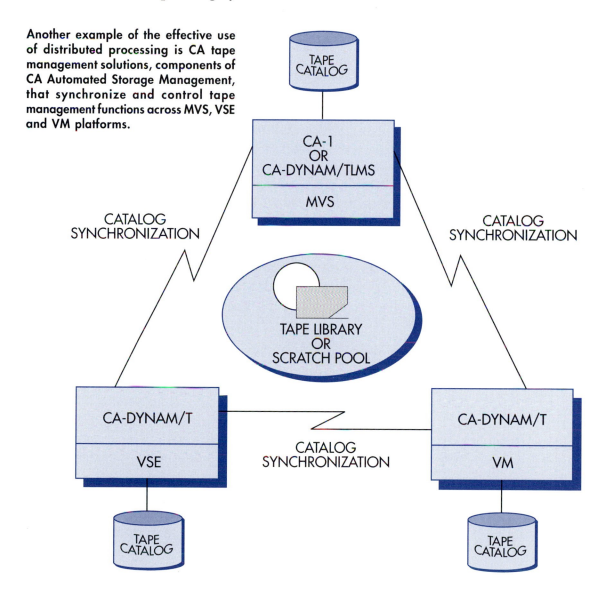

The client-server architecture is a very powerful way of structuring the internal components of an application that operates in both distributed and centralized configurations. Some components of the application, acting as clients, request services from other components acting as servers. The application works the same way when operating within a single system or with components spread over a network. Consider CA-1, the automated storage management system, which exploits this architecture to gain portability to different kinds of environments. In this case, a business application such as Masterpiece, the CA financial management system, is a client of CA-1, which acts as a server—but CA-1 also uses the client-server architecture internally. Requests for tape mounts, repository retrieval requests and operator interaction requests are processed by the appropriate server module, which may be operating far from the component originating the request—or all within a single mainframe. CA90s services, such as the Common Communication Interface, CAICCI, which provide the foundation for the client-server architecture, operate identically regardless of the environment.

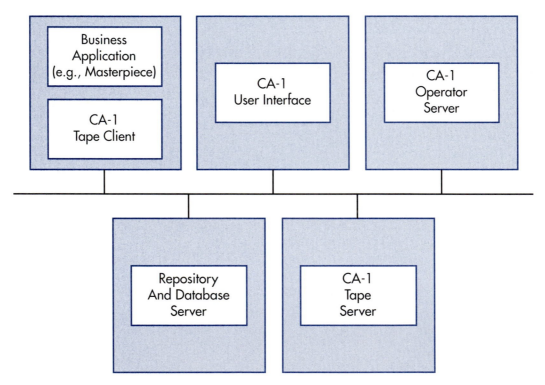

Client-server architecture, used internally within a solution such as CA-1, makes the solution independent of the system configuration: a business application requests a file, and the various function requests that CA-1 issues—check repository for business rules pertaining to archival of the file, request operator intervention to mount a tape, read the tape—are sent to server components which may operate within a single mainframe or on systems spread across a network. CAICCI and other foundation services operate identically regardless of the environment.

Summary

The complex and diverse challenges of information systems management today require the breadth of software functionality and the unique services of CA90s. The problems cannot be solved with niche solutions, whether the niche is one particular function, or one particular operating system. Effective service-level management cannot be performed without the ability to connect information from and control many diverse platforms and operating environments.

All Systems Management Software must work in concert to maintain a steady flow of throughput, and to respond quickly and accurately, with a minimum of wasted time and effort, to any disruption of the enterprise information processing environment.

The need to provide improved service with controlled costs requires that key personnel be utilized as effectively as possible. Total data center automation must be achieved to enable personnel to move away from constant monitoring of the computer system so that they can better analyze present and future information processing needs.

Computer Associates Systems Management Software solutions help IS management maximize the return on IS investment and achieve the total data center automation that ensures consistent service levels are maintained. These solutions offer unprecedented functionality and a level of integration across multiple operating systems and hardware platforms that no other vendor can offer. These capabilities result from a broad product line of interoperable, industry-leading solutions that exemplify the unique guiding principles and design of CA90s.

CHAPTER 7

Information Management Software

The Information Management Software Challenges

The information management area poses very different, yet no less challenging issues and concerns for IS management than those found in the systems management arena.

Information systems professionals need to be able to take advantage of the wealth of new technological breakthroughs aimed at helping to speed application development, manage data and applications, and allow efficient access to enterprise-wide information. This must be accomplished without sacrificing the substantial investments already made in existing data, applications and computing technology. Integrating new technology with existing, proven production applications is an absolute requirement of information management today.

In addition to the emergence of new technologies, the industry has witnessed the evolution of computing standards. These standards promise to add discipline and consistency to application development activities, helping to improve their quality. Yet, not only must these standards be applied to new applications to be effective, they must also be able to add value to the applications and computing environments that already exist.

Information management also requires the effective integration of the potent processing power available in desktop systems into the enterprise's overall information systems strategy. These less expensive but versatile systems offer enterprises cost-effective processing power through cooperative and distributed processing environments.

CA Information Management Software Meets These Challenges

Information Management Software from Computer Associates, incorporating the architecture and guiding principles of CA90s, effectively addresses these issues by providing the latest data management and platform-independent software engineering technologies, and by enabling enterprises to benefit from modern applications without discarding existing applications or duplicating existing data.

Information Management Software also forms the basis for the Database Management Services of the Integration Services layer of CA90s. This dual capacity, as standalone facilities and as CA90s services, enables CA clients who utilize Information Management Software to develop and enhance their own applications, thereby extending the inherent advantages of CA90s to the enterprise's vast portfolio of applications both old and new.

CA Information Management Software encompasses the data management functions of Database Management Systems and Dictionary/Repository Support as well as extensive Software Engineering capabilities (including Life Cycle Management and Application Development Systems).

CA Information Management Software encompasses the data management functions of database and dictionary/repository as well as extensive software engineering capabilities (including life cycle management and application development systems).

Database Management Systems

Relational database technology offers many important benefits, such as flexibility in data access, that have fueled an evolution from the extensive implementation of traditional database management systems to relational technology. Relational databases are widely used and appreciated for their convenience in end-user query and reporting and for their ease of comprehension and use in application development.

However, this technology has several shortcomings that prohibit it from being utilized strictly as a standalone solution. No purely relational technology provides all the facilities needed to support the most demanding transaction processing applications. For this reason, relational technology will only enjoy limited production usage, mostly in information center applications. Furthermore, in most cases clients have tremendous investments in production applications based on traditional database technology that forms the basis for their entire organization's information processing.

Enterprises wishing to derive the benefits of relational technology face the daunting prospect of either completely rewriting applications to use the new technology or operating multiple database management systems. Rewriting applications is not only prohibitively expensive and difficult, it also results in a loss of functionality due to SQL-based relational technology's inability to provide the many varied database functions that are required by most enterprises. The "dual database" approach is expensive and unwieldy and ensures the risk of inconsistency due to the already proven difficulty of maintaining duplicate data.

Both approaches, the complete migration to relational and the dual database, pose an important question about the future: when new data access techniques gain prominence, such as semantic or object orientation, will additional databases need to be supported? Will applications need to be rewritten again? This is a realistic concern and industry experts and researchers are actively studying these next generation technologies. SQL is not the final word.

CA's Unique Single Database Strategy Protects Investments

Computer Associates offers clients a better alternative: the ability to provide multiple data access techniques within a single database. This unique, "single database" strategy provides valuable investment protection. Clients have the flexibility to run existing applications and data that utilize navigational access techniques, add relational capabilities to existing applications, or build new applications using either navigational, relational or a combination of both access methods. This flexibility is achieved through the addition of SQL technology to the powerful, proven CA Database Management Systems, as well as through the use of transparency software.

Transparency software protects clients' investments in applications written for VSAM, IMS DL/I, DB2 and Cincom's TOTAL. The data needed for these applications is managed by the CA Database Management Systems and is also available for use by new applications. The database supports simultaneous access to the data through the transparency service and SQL or other database access methods. *Users do not have to rewrite existing applications, or use duplicate data.*

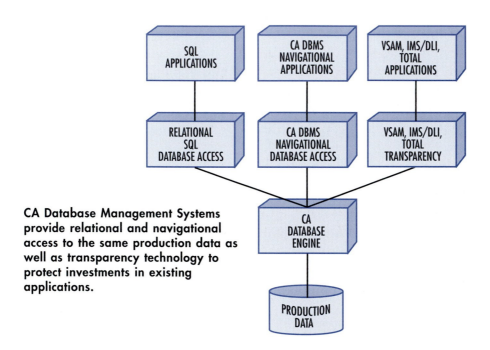

CA Database Management Systems provide relational and navigational access to the same production data as well as transparency technology to protect investments in existing applications.

As new ways to access data such as multimedia text, video and graphics are developed, they can be quickly and easily incorporated into the CA single database management strategy.

Computer Associates Information Management Software also helps enterprises effectively integrate midrange and desktop processing into the overall information systems strategy. CA Information Management Software enables the engineering of portable applications that are engineered to fully exploit the particular hardware and operating environment of each platform. This enables optimum computing performance on the system best suited for the task.

Computer Associates is the only vendor to extend proven database management technology by integrating the high-production processing capabilities of navigational access with the flexible ad hoc query facilities of relational access in a single database management system.

Computer Associates Database Management Systems are currently the basis for millions of mission-critical production systems for commercial and government organizations, while delivering the most flexible information access and end-user computing environment available.

Dictionary/Repository Support

For the last decade, CA active dictionaries have enabled the integration of database management systems with software engineering, bringing together business modeling and front-end CASE tools with application development systems and data modeling. The result is a significant increase in productivity and improvement in application quality.

Today, CA active dictionaries account for more than half of the data dictionary market. They already utilize the entity-relationship model that is now the standard for data modeling used by many front-end CASE products and has been adopted by the IBM Repository Manager/MVS. They enable the storing, maintaining and cross-referencing of data as well as impact analysis for more functions than the repository planned by IBM. The entity-relationship capability is also fully extensible, enabling enterprises to add their own entities and relate them to entities that exist already within the dictionaries.

This proven dictionary technology is the foundation for CA Repository Services. Repository Services let users manage and control all enterprise information, for Information Management as well as for CA Systems Management and Business Applications Software. It is also compatible with hardware vendor repositories such as IBM Repository Manager/MVS and Digital CDD/Repository.

CA Database Management Systems and Repository Services also play an active role in the CA90s Integration Services layer, supporting all CA Enterprise Software Solutions. The technology underlying Database Management Systems and Repository Services is more fully explained in Chapter 4.

Software Engineering

CA Information Management Software provides the most comprehensive software engineering solutions available, covering two essential categories: Life Cycle Management Systems for *managing* the job of software engineering and Application Development Systems for *performing* the job of software engineering.

Life Cycle Management Systems include extensive administrative tools for planning, designing, controlling and reporting on applications, application components, versions, configurations, tasks, resources, tools, people, schedules and costs.

Application Development Systems include a wide range of technical tools such as languages, code generators and nonprocedural systems, as well as services such as knowledge-based systems, panel managers, report managers, query managers and help managers.

Together, these two categories provide clients with the ability to quickly and accurately plan, build and maintain the flexible and productive applications they need to support their business activities.

Life Cycle Management

Effective Life Cycle Management provides automation and integration of the many, formerly separate tasks required to build large and small applications, including the following integrated components:

Project management—Developers are provided with integrated tools for estimation, planning and tracking of projects and management tools for controlling tasks, schedules, staff, resources and costs. The integrated project management tools from CA also utilize Graphics and Reporting Services to simplify analysis of the interdependencies of project steps and to better communicate the project requirements to managers, customers and others.

Desktop workstations provide great value in the area of project management, regardless of whether the development project is mainframe- or workstation-oriented. They provide a convenient user interface and graphical functions well-suited to the requirements of project management, particularly the use of multiple "what-if" scenarios to resolve resource or scheduling problems. The mainframe, however, offers superior power for large projects. Some developers use a mainframe as a consolidation station, bringing together subplans developed on workstations into a master plan on the mainframe, utilizing the superior power of the mainframe for large-scale tabular and graphical reporting. CA project management solutions support both of these configurations.

Front-end CASE solutions—The problem with many front-end Computer Aided Software Engineering (CASE) tools is their lack of integration with back-end database management and application development systems. CA front-end CASE solutions are fully integrated with CA Database Management Services, CA Dictionary/Repository Services and CA Application Development Systems. In addition, they provide an open architecture that supports major CASE tools from other vendors. Computer Associates also provides its own workstation-based graphical design tools for database and process design, closely integrated with dictionary models and back-end systems.

Configuration management—Applications comprise many components including program modules, database statements, SQL plans, schemas and subschemas, reports, panels, help text, messages, etc. Programs exist in the form of source code, compiled object code and linked executables. All these components must be managed during the life cycle of the application as it is designed, developed, tested, corrected, released, maintained, redesigned, reimplemented and rereleased. The resources used during development, such as data storage for program modules, must also be managed for efficiency, to improve the productivity of the developers and to reduce computer resource consumption. Library management, change control, version management and release generation play important roles in configuration management.

Complete development environment—Capabilities are provided for online, interactive development environments where programmers can move efficiently through the development process, including capabilities for testing, debugging and generation of test data; optimizing code to save machine resources; and PC workstation support to provide offline PC capabilities fully compatible with mainframe systems.

Computer Associates integrated Life Cycle Management Systems support the entire software engineering job, from analysis and design to maintenance and production management. The Life Cycle Management functions are not only integrated with each other, but with the repository/dictionaries which maintain information about all components of the Application Development Systems. In addition, CA90s supports an open architecture, allowing Life Cycle Management Systems to incorporate the utilization of third-party tools and services.

As an example of the integration provided by CA Life Cycle Management solutions, CA front-end CASE solutions are fully integrated with CA Database Management Systems, CA Dictionary/Repository Support and CA Application Development Systems. In addition, they provide an open architecture that supports major CASE tools from other vendors.

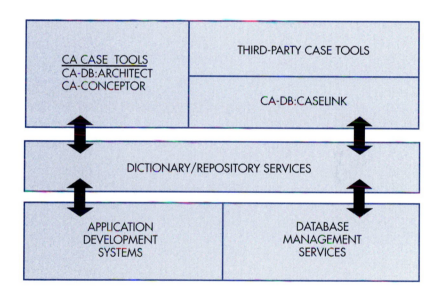

Application Development Systems

The real challenges in application development lie in raising productivity and building portable applications for complex computing environments without sacrificing industrial-level performance. At the same time, it is important that the right tool can be matched to the appropriate development task.

Computer Associates Information Management Software is unsurpassed in addressing these requirements by providing a comprehensive set of integrated, portable and open application development systems. These systems, fully integrated with the CA dictionary/repository services, library management systems and CA Standard Security Facility, include the following integrated tools to satisfy the varied development needs of every enterprise:

Fourth-Generation Languages—high-level languages whose high-speed development facilities can create both small systems and demanding, critical, "industrial strength" transaction processing applications.

Code generators—very high-level, nonprocedural application generation systems that ensure the highest operating performance by relying on established third- or fourth-generation languages for execution.

Nonprocedural, rule-based systems—powerful, high-productivity development techniques especially suited for prototyping applications due to their ability to show not only the appearance, but also the behavior of an application.

Expert systems—the Application Services' knowledge-based systems that include support for voice technology integrated into the processing and database environment of commercial applications to address their complex decision making requirements.

Query systems—high-level systems for easy end-user access to host data to satisfy ad hoc query, simple applications and basic data management needs.

Extensive COBOL development tools—including integrated tools with facilities for COBOL testing and optimization, source management and change control, CICS testing and debugging, workstation environment, COBOL code generation, COBOL-based graphics, and test data generation.

In line with the open architecture of CA Application Development Systems, CA provides productivity tools specifically aimed at DB2 environments. These tools include a fourth-generation language that delivers improved productivity, ease of use and complete integration with DB2; a nonprocedural tool, incorporating the dBASE language, that handles quick prototyping and creation of queries and applications for production or information center use; facilities for automatic database design and process modeling that links vendor CASE tools with fourth-generation languages and DB2; and a structured COBOL code generator that improves the efficiency and maintainability of COBOL programs on DB2.

As an example of Computer Associates commitment to providing multiple platform support, high-performance VAX tools are also available including comprehensive tools for database management and application development (including code generators and CA90s Application Services expert systems that utilize DECvoice response technology) in the VAX/VMS environment. Computer Associates also provides a high-performance, production VAX database management system.

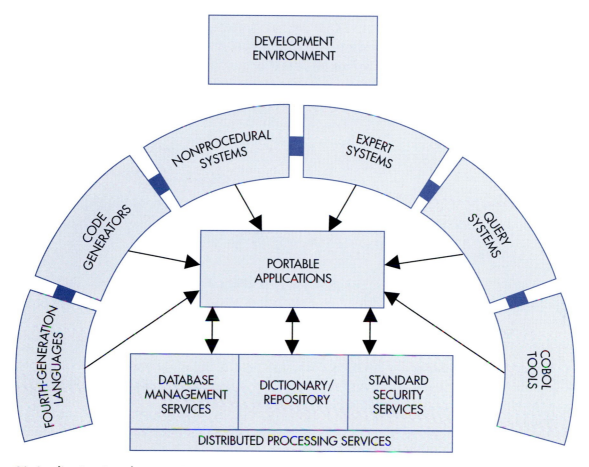

CA Application Development Systems comprise many integrated tools that can be matched to the appropriate development task. These systems are fully integrated with CA90s Integration Services and Distributed Processing Services, providing superior application portability across multiple operating environments.

CA90s And Information Management Software

CA90s adds substantial value to the data management and software engineering solutions within the Information Management Software area. The applications that CA clients build using CA Information Management Software, as well as the CA solutions built using the same technology, gain significant benefits from the layered architecture and the services.

Multi-Platform Capabilities

Multi-platform capabilities in Information Management Software provide important benefits: they allow clients to use desktop systems as development workstations for lower cost and higher productivity, and they allow clients to migrate applications to many different kinds of systems and to develop enterprise-wide applications. This entails both "downsizing," moving applications from mainframes to PCs, LANs or midrange systems to exploit the better price/performance of these smaller systems and the use of a mix of systems for the same application in order to choose the optimal configuration for each business location.

Both CA Application Development Systems and the underlying database foundation are architected for portability across multiple platforms. For example, applications built with high-level languages such as CA-IDEAL and CA-ADS may be moved *unchanged* to MVS, VSE, VM, VMS, UNIX and PC environments. The application generator CA-DB:GENERATOR can generate systems in COBOL, C, FORTRAN, BASIC or CA-ADS and the originating program specification rules are portable not only across platforms but also across database management systems.

CA Database Management Systems, CA-IDMS, CA-DATACOM and CA-DB, provide relational SQL access and native navigational access across all the platforms mentioned above, ensuring that not only the application logic is portable but that database structures and database operations are portable as well.

Both database management systems and application development systems, such as CA-IDMS/PC and CA-ADS/PC as well as CA-DATACOM/PC and CA-IDEAL/PC, support not only PC environments but LAN environments in client-server organizations.

"Portability," as defined by CA90s, is not simply the migration of the same code to additional platforms. Database and application development systems, which are used for mission critical applications, must be engineered to optimize the performance on each particular platform. CA Information Management Software provides compatibility in the *external interface* for portability, while utilizing environment-specific *internal technology* for performance.

Downsizing

Downsizing, the movement of work to smaller systems, takes many forms which pose different requirements for the Information Management Software. As the needs of Information Systems users evolve to increasing levels of sophistication, the CA90s services and technologies provide the CA Information Management solutions with the foundation for meeting these needs.

Offloading development to smaller systems, often PCs, requires a completely compatible environment: databases, languages and applications.

Compatible databases: Applications written for mainframe database management systems should be able to move to smaller systems using the same data structures and the same access methods. While SQL offers many practical benefits, information systems professionals should be able to make the decision about when and how to utilize relational processing independently of the move to new systems.

Compatible languages: Business applications are traditionally written in languages such as COBOL, CA-ADS and CA-IDEAL. While the evangelists of the new technologies preach the advantages of C, C++ and Modula2, the move to new systems should not require the obsolescence of either the application solutions or the expertise of application development staff.

Compatible applications: Even more important than preserving the expertise of the technical staff is leveraging the investment in training of end users. Since people often move between offices, using different systems, applications should be consistent across platforms. While minor variations are acceptable, the overall behavior and philosophy of the application should remain consistent.

Application testing: a crucial step in all development, requires that we expand the meaning of the word "compatible" to include not only the syntax, but the semantics and the functions of the system as well. The PC development workstation must not impose size constraints, on the application or its database, which may render real world applications untestable in the workstation environment. The application development and database management systems support an equally strong dictionary on the smaller development system to allow the application to be moved intact between development and production systems.

Downsizing production applications requires the same compatibility, in order to allow existing production applications to be migrated to the smaller platform without change. Production execution may target a midrange system, such as a UNIX and VAX machine, or a network of smaller systems running PC-DOS or UNIX. To meet the performance, data-sharing, integrity and security needs of production applications, the Information Management Software fully supports Local Area Networks, provides database server support, and exploits the platform for optimum performance.

Exploiting the platform by tailoring production applications to the special characteristics of the hardware requires built-in support for graphical user interfaces, the advanced functions of laser printers, and other special facilities such as the Dynamic Data Exchange (DDE) of Windows. While tailoring the application implies change, this tailoring should require no unnecessary changes: compatibility is still important to minimize the effort and retraining involved in exploiting the platform. For example, the complexities of programming for the graphical user interface environment should be minimized, allowing the preservation of the general structure of the application and much of its user interfacing detail. CA high-level development systems will simplify GUI development just as they simplify pseudoconversational development on the mainframe.

User Interface and Visualization Services

The User Interface and Visualization Services provide consistent interaction between the human being and the computer, and help CA Information Management Software satisfy the demands of end users in the 90s. These services are used by and made available to CA clients through CA Application Development Systems such as CA-DB:GENERATOR.

The User Interface Management Services (CAIUIMS) provide applications with powerful user interfacing functions aimed at improving the productivity and reducing the learning curve of application end users. CAIUIMS is utilized as a supporting service in the CA Application Development Systems, simplifying the task of developing modern applications through its provision for data formatting, input validation, pop-up choice list management, help and message management, as well as navigation through pull-down menus, function keys, etc. CAIUIMS supports graphical user interfaces in a transparent manner, allowing applications designed for portability to exploit the capabilities of graphical workstations without burdening the developer with separately maintaining a block mode, a character mode and a GUI version of an application.

The Reporting Services are also used in Application Development Systems, providing applications with a high-level report definition and testing system for simplified development together with the high-quality output of the advanced function printer support.

Voice Services are also integrated with the CA-DB:EXPERT application development system, providing this sophisticated form of user interfacing to applications using one of the several supported database management systems.

Distributed Processing Services

Various forms of distributed processing are becoming essential in many of the mission-critical applications of the 90s executing on mainframe and midrange networks, on PC LANs, and in PC-host configurations.

CA Database Management Systems support several forms of distributed processing, including both the advanced distributed database processing of CA-DB:STAR and the remote database server facilities available through CA-IDMS/DB and CA-DATACOM/DB between mainframes, CA-DB/VAX and CA-DB/UNIX in midrange environments and CA-IDMS/PC and CA-DATACOM/PC in LAN environments.

Application-level cooperative processing is supported through CA Application Development Systems which utilize the powerful functions in the Distributed Processing Services layer of CA90s.

Integration Services

The Integration Services of CA90s provide applications with several important benefits, some very visible and some less obvious. Among the most important is the CA Standard Security Facility (CAISSF) which provides security integration and centralized security administration for both database and application development systems. This service allows access control for both the development process and the production execution of the application to be administered through the standard security administration tools of the site, including database security administration.

Another important service is the CA SQL Interface (CAISQI) which is provided through the Database Management Services. CAISQI provides a transparent interface to several database management systems including those from third parties, and is the foundation technology which allows solutions built with CA Application Development Systems to be executed with DB2, Rdb, Oracle or CA databases without change.

The applications that users build utilizing CA Information Management Software will gain all of the benefits of the CA90s Services.

USER-WRITTEN APPLICATIONS

USER INTERFACE & VISUALIZATION SERVICES

ENTERPRISE SOFTWARE SOLUTIONS

INTEGRATION SERVICES

DISTRIBUTED PROCESSING SERVICES

PLATFORMS

SOFTWARE ENGINEERING

LIFE CYCLE MANAGEMENT

APPLICATION DEVELOPMENT

DATA MANAGEMENT

Summary

Information Management Software successfully meets the challenges of the 90s, satisfying productivity, flexibility and portability demands while protecting investments in existing applications. New technologies such as relational database and nonprocedural application generation can benefit an enterprise immeasurably, but only if their benefits are not diminished by the need to rewrite existing applications or run an inefficient and expensive dual database environment. CA90s brings information processing advances into the established world of proven technologies, integrating the new techniques with existing systems and offering the best of both relational and navigational worlds.

CA90s Information Management Software not only provides advanced technology for building applications but also goes one step beyond, by addressing the complex needs of managing the entire application life cycle, from analysis and design through implementation, release and maintenance. These Life Cycle Management systems are enhanced by their association with CA90s Integration Services such as the Standard Security Facility.

CA90s Information Management Software protects clients' investments in current and future applications by providing multiple platform support, allowing the evolution of applications into enterprise-wide solutions across mainframe, midrange and desktop systems. Integration with the User Interface and Visualization Services multiplies the value of these applications by allowing them to exploit the capabilities of graphical workstations, voice interfacing and advanced laser printers. The availability of fully compatible languages and Database Management Services allows the use of desktop systems as development workstations, lowering costs and improving productivity.

By drawing on the power of the Distributed Processing Services, the Database Management and Application Development Systems provide a foundation for distributed solutions, providing transparent distributed database processing as well as application-level cooperative processing for mainframe, midrange, workstation and LAN environments.

The powerful technologies inherent in CA Information Management Software are extended tremendously by the Service Layers of CA90s to help bring enterprise solutions into the demanding computing environments of the 90s.

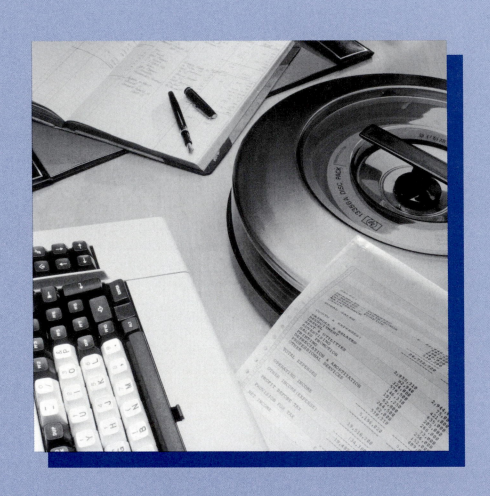

CHAPTER 8

Business Applications
Software

The Business Applications Software Challenges

Never before have businesses been faced with such demanding business challenges: the global economy, high competitive pressure, the necessity to control costs and business decentralization. Timely response to these challenges can enable an enterprise to establish and sustain strategic advantage over the competition and support the achievement of its business objectives; failure to respond can relegate a business to stagnation or worse.

Opportunity for expansion into new foreign markets has never been greater. With this new global marketplace comes the challenges of dealing with multiple languages, multiple currencies, and differing accounting and government regulatory requirements. Even corporations with entirely domestic operations may buy or sell in foreign currency, requiring currency conversion.

Global competition on the other hand only increases the ever-growing competitive pressure most corporations face. This pressure demands flexibility and responsiveness within all levels of the enterprise. Rapid recognition and reaction to each new business opportunity is the key to maintaining the edge over one's competition. But each new opportunity also involves potentially costly risks. To miss an opportunity is to become a victim of progress; risks must be minimized to assure success.

Enterprises also look to achieve greater efficiency and control over their business operations in order to improve profitability. Controlling costs through increased automation, improved productivity and the incorporation of new, more cost-effective technology are primary ways in which an enterprise's profitability can be improved.

Many firms are finding that the traditional centralized operations of the past limit their ability to adequately address the competitive and cost pressures they face today. Decentralization of their operations can allow more local control over market conditions. A retailer, for instance, may decentralize to accommodate regional buying preferences and merchandising styles. This in turn, reduces inventory levels, delivery times, and delivery costs; all of which improve profitability.

CA Business Applications Software Meets These Challenges

Computer Associates Business Applications Software, incorporating the architecture and guiding principles of CA90s, provides superior solutions that address these challenges. CA Business Applications offer clients an extensive set of specialized functions integrated with each other and with the unique services of CA90s that enables the software to effectively support the needs of an enterprise as it strives to achieve its objectives.

CA Business Applications Software automates a broad range of business functions. From the Generally Accepted Accounting Principles (GAAP)-dictated "standard" financial management products for monitoring and reporting activity to more focused industry-specific solutions, CA Business Applications provide unmatched functionality and flexibility in meeting user needs.

With the increasingly international nature of modern business, most organizations need international business application solutions. Organizations with multi-national operations require applications with user interfaces that support multiple languages; formats for numbers, dates and addresses; and flexibility in calculation routines to handle differing taxations and legislative requirements. Support for multiple currencies and currency conversions are becoming minimum requirements for any corporation that does business with foreign companies. These requirements are addressed today in CA multi-national Business Applications Software.

To effectively address today's mounting competitive pressure, Information Systems must provide responsive and flexible analysis capabilities. Accuracy of information used for decision making is essential to successfully capitalize on new opportunities. The use of an integrated database in CA Business Applications Software addresses these needs through flexible relational database technology combined with query, reporting, analysis and graphics tools for decision support.

Business applications are a primary means for enterprises to control costs. CA Business Applications' usage of high-performance database and transaction processing systems results in excellent operating efficiency of the applications themselves. The integrated application design allows a greater degree of automation in processing, resulting in fewer redundant activities and less manual involvement. This not only improves initial productivity, but also reduces business errors and their associated rework. Consistent use of modern user interfaces by CA Business Applications improves end-user productivity and significantly reduces training costs.

Through a foundation of database management systems and high-level languages which are portable to multiple platforms, CA Business Applications give an enterprise the flexibility to choose the most cost-effective system for each circumstance and each processing load. This decision can be made today with the knowledge that these same business applications will be able to take advantage of new, radically different computing technology advances in the future, thus enabling the enterprise to realize the efficiency gains and cost benefits these technologies can bring. In addition to traditional business systems from IBM and Digital (MVS, VSE, OS/400 and VMS) the CA Business Applications are aimed at UNIX systems to take advantage of the open systems movement.

Business decentralization often brings the need to decentralize the associated information processing for both operational and cost-effectiveness reasons. This can take the form of both fully decentralized processing or a combination of centralized and decentralized processing (distributed processing). CA Business Applications provide this functionality through multiple platform support (including PC and LAN-based systems), distributed processing (both cooperative processing and distributed database support), and LAN-based client-server architectures.

CA Business Applications Software offers a broad range of integrated functions designed to support the needs of an enterprise as it strives to achieve its objectives.

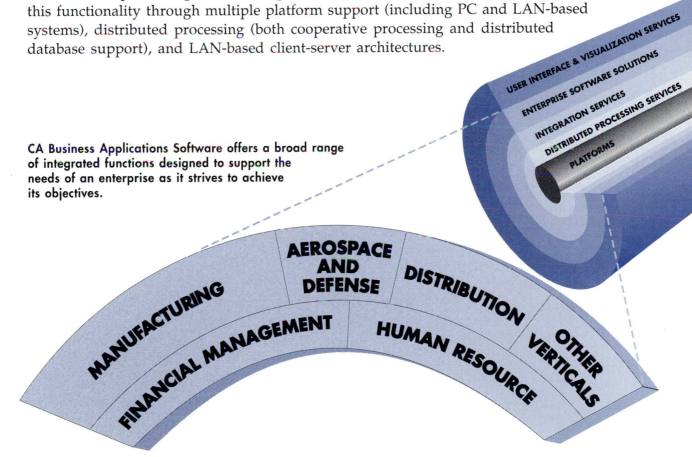

CA Business Applications Software addresses both vertical and horizontal markets and includes the following:

Financial Management Software

CA Financial Management Software comprises integrated solutions including horizontal solutions such as general ledger, accounts payable, accounts receivable, collection and recovery, purchasing, inventory control, order processing, fixed assets, financial consolidation, financial modeling, job costing and labor distribution.

A highly specialized, vertical solution included in Financial Management Software is fund/encumbrance accounting. It provides realtime control over specific fund expenditures as they apply to not-for-profit organizations such as schools, hospitals and municipalities.

The Financial Management Software enables users to integrate, consolidate and control the various functions of their business across a broad range of operating system and hardware platforms. Common tools for accessing, inquiring and reporting on the financial information contained within the enterprise's Information Systems are available. The flexible software solutions also provide comprehensive realtime and batch accounting functions that include complementary decision support and graphic presentation tools to ensure a cohesive, integrated solution.

CA Financial Management solutions address the widely differing needs of enterprises of different types and sizes, ranging from PC and LAN-based systems for smaller organizations to comprehensive solutions for midrange and mainframe systems.

Human Resource Management Software

Human Resource Management Software includes a comprehensive, integrated group of solutions with personnel management, payroll, applicant tracking and position control functions.

Payroll departments must maintain consistent performance while accommodating change and growth. Personnel departments must create new ways of attracting, motivating and retaining highly qualified employees. Management must be able to track and report on the flow of job applicants and applications.

The CA Human Resource Management Software utilizes a common database to ensure an integrated solution that enables payroll and personnel information to be efficiently utilized as a corporate-wide resource.

Manufacturing Management Software

Computer Associates Manufacturing Management Software serves manufacturers in the discrete and repetitive environments, as well as those in the aerospace and defense industries. This completely integrated solution provides support for bill of material, cost control, forecast management, order entry, distribution requirements planning, inventory control, material requirements planning, master production scheduling, shop floor control and purchasing management.

These proven solutions have helped many of the most well-respected manufacturers achieve world-class status. Just-In-Time (JIT) methodologies for managing manufacturing operations incorporated as a part of these systems help to deliver quality improvements and cost reductions necessary to achieve this status.

Distribution Management Software

CA Distribution Management Software offers a full range of integrated distribution management capabilities for effective control of logistics and warehouse management. It automates the information processing requirements of finished goods and inventory distribution for medium-sized and large companies.

Distribution Management Software combines forecasting and distribution requirements planning (DRP) functions to reduce inventory and carrying costs. The effective management of distribution centers satisfies customer demand through an online order management process, and increases overall warehouse productivity through physical inventory storage and materials handling management facilities which exploit the latest in warehouse management hardware technologies.

CA90s and Business Applications Software

CA Business Applications Software receives extensive benefits from incorporating the architecture and guiding principles of CA90s. The very nature of the CA90s layered architectural approach allows the Business Applications to exploit the services provided by the architecture outside of the functional business processing of the applications themselves. This allows the Business Applications to rapidly respond to and implement new, powerful and cost-effective technology without compromising the integrity of the actual business application functions. Additionally, as the services embedded in these layers provide insulation from platform specific hardware and operating system characteristics, the Business Applications inherit most of their portability requirements simply through the use of these services. The result of the use of CA90s services is Business Applications Software that protects clients' investment in business processing functionality while exploiting in the quickest fashion possible ever-advancing technology changes—an unparalleled combination of stability and flexibility.

Use of the Service Layers also enables CA Business Applications Software to provide consistent functionality and "look and feel" among applications and across platforms. This allows a branch office, for example, with a desktop or midrange system to treat an invoice, an order or an employee in the same way as headquarters does with a mainframe. Consistency between applications and across platforms reduces training costs and enhances productivity of all users.

Integration between Business Applications systems themselves allows the extension of functionality across traditional business area boundaries with the significant benefit of improved productivity. Additionally, through the CA90s Integration Services, the Business Applications Software is also integrated with solutions provided in the Computer Associates Systems Management and Information Management Software, functions such as security facilities available in CA Systems Management Software and application development tools available in CA Information Management Software. This level of integration forms *unique combinations of functionality difficult to match in other business applications solutions.*

More effective utilization of an enterprise's total computing resources by Business Applications Software is also achieved by use of CA90s services. For example, through the use of CA90s Distributed Processing Services, business processing can occur on the most responsive and cost-effective machine resource available within the enterprise.

User Interface and Visualization Services

CA Business Applications are designed specifically for end users and, as such, utilize many of the user-friendly capabilities of the User Interface and Visualization Services. These services provide a consistent "look and feel" for users of CA Business Applications Software. In IBM environments, the User Interface and Visualization Services support the Common User Access (CUA) guidelines defined in IBM's SAA initiative. Users in the Digital VAX environment will have the option of electing to use the Network Application Support (NAS) standard or CUA.

A consistent "look and feel" allows people to move from system to system, performing the same function on different systems without requiring retraining. This is fundamental to the efficient use of staff, particularly in a decentralized environment. The "look and feel," while consistent across applications and platforms, should not, however, be based on the lowest common denominator. For ease of use and efficiency, CA Business Applications make use of the specific capabilities of each system, such as high bandwidth interactivity and graphics on desktop systems. However, the philosophy and semantics of each system, as well as the flow and procedures of operating them, are the same.

A fundamental philosophy recognized by CA Business Applications is that computer systems are there to help, not control, the user. For example, if an application requires the entry of one out of a list of specific values, such as a department name, the system should not just verify that a legitimate value is entered and notify the user of errors, but also, on request, provide a list of valid entries and allow the user to select one.

The use of menus and lists of objects to select from (such as account numbers, vendors and products) makes the system easier and more efficient to use: recognition is easier than recall, selection is easier than typing, and both reduce error rates. The ability to use commands, function keys and other shortcuts ensures speedy processing for the expert. The combination of functional actions, menus backed by shortcuts, commands and data entry fields backed by prompt pop-up menus, is provided by CA90s and offers the best of both worlds.

CA-MASTERSTATION

CA-MASTERSTATION, a cooperative processing workstation for Masterpiece (CA financial software), offers a common "look and feel" through a standard interface that follows IBM CUA guidelines in mainframe, midrange and workstation environments.

Business Applications Software also takes advantage of the strong capabilities that graphics bring to the end user. Graphics applications significantly enhance the presentation and understanding of data for all business application reporting. In our modern, information-rich and fast-moving business environment, more and more companies are required to analyze, digest and act on increasingly larger volumes of information. The enterprises most effectively meeting these challenges are often using new information systems to help them cope. Business graphics are ideal tools to supplement standard reporting to quickly and clearly communicate important decision-making information.

Integration Services

The very nature of business application information lends itself to database implementations. Varied views of application information are required on a daily basis by most organizations.

Unlike many other offerings of business software, Computer Associates Business Applications are built on a solid foundation of database management systems. This foundation uniquely offers high performance, operating reliability, protection of data integrity against loss or corruption of data through accident or malfeasance, and convenience and flexibility in query, reporting and customization.

Masterpiece, the Computer Associates integrated financial management application solution, is delivered with full relational database management system capabilities through the utilization of the Integration Services layer of CA90s. In addition, the single database management approach of CA90s enables the coexistence of relational and navigational access techniques providing unmatched flexibility and performance capabilities. Because of the open architecture of CA90s, Masterpiece also allows implementation in a VSAM or DB2 data management environment.

A database foundation including dictionary/repository functionality also gives business applications integration capabilities that enable enterprise information to be available as a single resource, giving client departments faster and more reliable access to consistent information. Changes made in one functional area are immediately reflected in all related areas. The applications can cooperate, for example, ensuring that goods have been both ordered correctly (Purchasing) and received in good condition (Inventory Control) before an invoice is approved for payment (Accounts Payable).

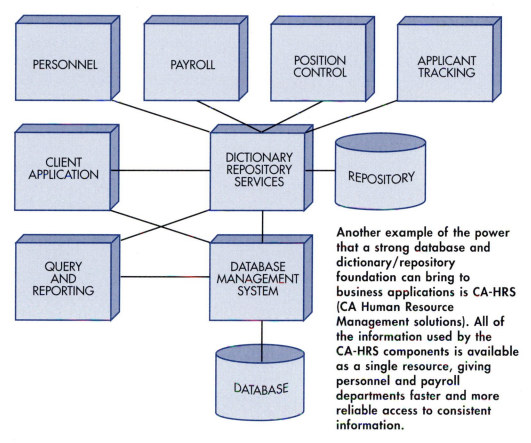

Another example of the power that a strong database and dictionary/repository foundation can bring to business applications is CA-HRS (CA Human Resource Management solutions). All of the information used by the CA-HRS components is available as a single resource, giving personnel and payroll departments faster and more reliable access to consistent information.

Query And Reporting Capabilities

Powerful CA query, report and analysis facilities can instantly retrieve, correlate and analyze all the data managed within the application system, without concern for the details of the data structure or application function boundaries. The consolidation of information from different applications (Order Processing, Material Requirements Planning, Purchasing, Inventory Control, Accounts Payable, etc.) in one integrated database produces a system in which users can create their own unique requests from any combination of information sources. The relational database model provides particularly extensive flexibility in combining data items for reporting.

Standard CA query and reporting tools also include PC-based facilities, which provide access to application data through the convenience of a PC-style user interface. They provide PC-based reporting and also allow export of application data to PC-based tools such as spreadsheets, graphics, etc. In some cases, subject to security restrictions, they even allow import of spreadsheet data into the application database.

Customization Capabilities

The placement of application data in a standard database also gives CA clients great flexibility in customizing the systems, extending them, and developing other applications integrated with CA Business Applications Software solutions. The customization facilities built into the database include the ability to tailor or extend data contents, to customize the system to match the individual configuration and work load for optimal performance, and to define integrity rules based on business policies.

The functionality of CA Business Applications Software may also be extended with custom applications working with the same data. Applications can use the database, extracting information for custom reporting, direct marketing, customer support, transaction validation or specialized calculations in external applications. In some cases data maintenance may even be done through external programs. Access to the database is supported through extensive CA application development systems. In all cases, access is controlled through the security facilities of the database management system.

Security Integration

Historically, Business Applications Software provided internal security mechanisms for defining users and controlling access to application-specific information and functions. With the trend toward enterprise-wide security control through external security systems such as CA-ACF2 and CA-TOP SECRET, these internal security systems have become "extra steps" in defining what an end user is authorized to do.

To simplify this process, CA Business Applications offer an option to centralize all security control through the use of the CA Standard Security Facility (CAISSF). This integration eliminates the duplication of effort and the attendant risk of error involved in maintaining multiple security systems.

Decision Support Integration

The information managed by the Business Applications can be a strategic asset, giving farsighted organizations a competitive advantage. This wealth of information lays a solid foundation for pro-active business management: strategic planning, analysis of sales by region, product and other categories, sales forecasting, customer support programs, direct marketing, etc. The data provides management with valuable insight into sales, contracts and costs; suppliers, customers and employees; products, components and raw materials; geographic patterns, distribution patterns and time patterns. Decision support capabilities, available from the CA90s Application Services, integrated with Business Applications Software provide enormous opportunities for better business management.

Some of the extensive services provided by decision support tools include:

- Query and reporting
- Spreadsheet
- Modeling and analysis

These decision support tools are available on larger systems (mainframe and midrange) and on desktop systems. Mainframe applications can transfer information directly to mainframe analysis and reporting tools, or download them to tools on a desktop workstation. For example, host-based budget and journal information can be accessed and analyzed with spreadsheet programs offering cross-platform capabilities.

Distributed Processing Services

CA90s Distributed Processing Services enable enterprises to deal with the challenges of supporting a distributed structure while maintaining the integrity of their business information. Having business applications software that meets these challenges allows an enterprise to choose the most responsive and cost-effective computing resource that will properly support their processing requirements.

Business Applications Software utilizes the Distributed Processing Services to support distributed database operation across mainframe and PC workstation environments. Support is further being extended to include other IBM and non-IBM platforms including midrange, desktop and LAN-based client-server architectures.

CA-CAS/DATA, a component of CA-CAS (CA Manufacturing Management Software), takes advantage of Distributed Processing Services for both consolidation and distribution of manufacturing information across mainframe, departmental midrange and desktop systems. Its open architecture also allows integration with third-party software through user-definable inputs.

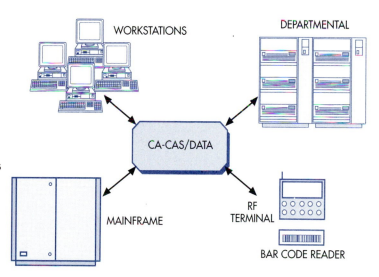

Cooperative Processing Services are also provided by the Distributed Processing Services layer. Utilization of Cooperative Processing Services allows tasks to be allocated to the computing platform that is most appropriate for the job and to platforms that provide a more cost-effective solution. A good example of cooperative processing for Business Applications Software is CA-MASTERSTATION, which serves as a graphical user interface to a host-based accounting system and adheres to CUA guidelines. Communication with the host is completely transparent to the CA-MASTERSTATION user. The Manufacturing and Human Resource management systems also provide workstations for moving suitable functions such as shop floor control and application tracking to a PC.

A very advanced form of distributed processing is used in CA-DMS, CA Distribution Management Software. Radio frequency technology is utilized to allow communications with the warehouse floor for picking, putaway, location replenishment and physical/cycle counting functions. Communications are established between a departmental system and hand-held or material handling equipment-mounted radio frequency devices including bar code entry devices. Through this technology, CA-DMS can direct the movements and priorities of the warehouse operation.

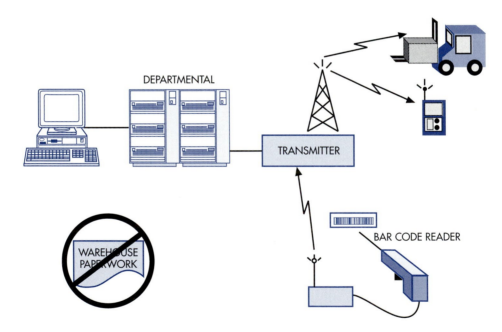

CA-DMS, CA Distribution Management Software, utilizes radio frequency technology to direct the movements and priorities of the warehouse operation.

Summary

Computer Associates provides integrated, flexible, comprehensive business application solutions that enable enterprises to utilize Information Systems effectively to achieve their business objectives.

Through their exploitation of CA90s Service Layers, CA Business Applications Software is continually incorporating the latest technology changes. These applications provide consistent functionality and "look and feel" between applications and platforms. They deliver a high level of integration among themselves, with Systems Management Software and with Information Management Software, and derive extensive benefits from a strong database foundation. In addition, Business Applications Software incorporates platform independence and distributed processing capabilities.

CA Business Applications Software is unmatched in the industry through its ability to rapidly exploit radically different technologies in order to achieve the highest efficiency, flexibility and functionality.

Modern user interfacing techniques, common across the entire spectrum of applications and operating platforms, ensures ease of use and reduces training costs.

The freedom to match the processing task to the system best suited for the job, as well as the ability to share processing cooperatively across multiple platforms, ensures the cost-effective use of valuable computing resources.

Flexibility, performance, reliability and functionality enable CA Business Applications Software to satisfy an enterprise's continually changing needs for timely and accurate business information.

CONCLUSION

Information systems are essential to enterprises and can provide competitive advantage in the highly charged business climate of the 90s. At the same time, they have become more complex and harder to manage than ever before. Technological advancements in hardware and software that have given rise to such trends as open systems architectures, distributed processing, client-server architectures, and more, have spawned multi-platform environments that create great opportunities, yet pose daunting challenges as well.

IS management is responsible for meeting the challenges of multi-platform environments and capitalizing on their benefits to positively impact the enterprise's ability to compete. By exploiting the new opportunities while leveraging investments already made in existing information systems, IS management can restore order to information systems.

CA90s is a software architecture designed to provide IS managers with the tools they need to achieve this order. With order, comes the ability to implement a cohesive information systems strategy that truly meets the business goals of the enterprise. CA90s also provides the flexibility required by the enterprise to modify the IS strategy as business needs and technology change, without disrupting the existing IS operations upon which the enterprise relies so heavily.

The Computing Architecture For The 90s is comprehensive; its benefits are not limited to a single "niche" area. CA90s provides for the development of integrated software solutions for every facet of information processing across multiple platform environments. These include the tools and languages used by application developers, the systems management software that supports data center operations and the business applications required to visibly improve the competitive position of the enterprise.

Unlike other architectures, CA90s builds upon the tremendous investments enterprises have already made in hardware, software and expertise. It serves as a framework for the evolutionary introduction of the latest technologies, ensuring the successful coexistence of new techniques and established ones.

CA90s is also a value-added architecture. It embraces the already widely accepted standards present in the industry today, extending them across multiple platform environments where needed in order to produce a cohesive view of computing.

CA90s is already evident in the hundreds of quality solutions and services offered by Computer Associates. While the full potential of CA90s has not yet been realized in every CA software solution, the technology, features and capabilities of the CA90s services are widely represented today, serving as examples of what will be.

Computer Associates is committed to bringing the benefits of the CA90s development blueprint and its guiding principles to all CA software solutions. Ultimately, CA90s is the only computing architecture that gives enterprises the freedom to choose the appropriate hardware platforms and software solutions for each aspect of their business, while enabling these technologies to be managed as an integrated whole.

GLOSSARY

Advanced Function Printing—Technology utilized by high-quality printers such as laser printers that produce near-typeset image quality output, supporting multiple typefaces, type sizes and type styles; proportionally spaced fonts; line drawings; shadings; graphics; etc. *See also* Reporting Services.

API—*See* Application Programming Interface.

Application Development Systems—The category of Software Engineering (a component of CA Information Management Software) that provides automated and integrated technical tools such as languages, code generators, CASE tools, nonprocedural systems and other services used to build software systems. *See also* Software Engineering and Information Management Software.

Application Programming Interface (API)—A well-defined set of functions or instructions that enable services to be easily shared by many programs, thus reducing redundancy in application design. Application programming interfaces are utilized by the components of CA90s. *See also* CA90s and Service Layers.

Application Services—Components of the Integration Services layer of CA90s that provide standard end-user functions for Enterprise Software Solutions such as single-point signon, single-point user registration, decision support, project management, change management, expert systems, product validation, C runtime, installation and maintenance, as well as service and support. *See also* Integration Services.

Application-to-Application Processing—Functionality provided by the Distributed Processing Services layer of CA90s that enables Enterprise Software Solutions on several systems, each performing application-level processing, to cooperate as partners in achieving a desired function. Also known as "peer-to-peer" processing. *See also* Cooperative Processing Services and Distributed Processing Services.

Architecture—A blueprint for software development that usually offers a standard set of services or common functions that can be invoked through a standard set of interfaces. *See also* CA90s, Systems Application Architecture and Network Application Support.

Automated Production Control Software—A comprehensive and integrated set of Systems Management Software that addresses the various areas of data center production activities including, production scheduling, rerun, restart and recovery, console management, report distribution, JCL validation, report balancing, and production documentation. *See also* Systems Management Software.

Automated Storage Management Software—A comprehensive and integrated set of Systems Management Software that addresses multimedia management, extended data management, and performance and reliability management for a variety of media across multiple platforms. *See also* Systems Management Software.

Business Applications Software—The segment of Enterprise Software Solutions that automates a broad range of business functions and provides advanced analytical capabilities. CA Business Applications Software includes Financial Management, Human Resource Management, Manufacturing Management and Distribution Management. *See also* Enterprise Software Solutions.

C Runtime Facility—A component of the Application Services that brings the C language compiler and runtime services typically available on desktop and midrange systems to mainframe software development environments. *See also* Application Services.

CA Extended SQL—An extension of the ANSI SQL standard for relational processing that provides a richer set of capabilities for accessing database management systems, and that serves as the application programming interface (API) to CA Database Management Services. *See also* Application Programming Interface, Relational Technology and Database Management Services.

CA Repository Services—*See* Repository Services

CA90s: Computing Architecture For The 90s—Computer Associates blueprint for a software architecture and its underlying guiding principles that provide an effective, comprehensive strategy for software development that meets the needs of the Information Systems community. *See also* Guiding Principles, Service Layers, Enterprise Software Solutions and Platforms.

CAGE—*See* Computer Associates Graphics Environment.

CASE—*See* Computer Aided Software Engineering.

CAICCI—*See* Common Communication Interface.

CAICRI—*See* Common Repository Interface.

CAIENF—*See* Event Notification Facility.

CAIPVI—*See* Product Validation Interface.

CAISSF—*See* Standard Security Facility.

CAISQI—*See* SQL Interface.

CAIUIMS—*See* User Interface Management Services.

Change Management Services—Components of the Application Services designed to record, analyze the impact of, approve and implement in a consistent fashion, changes to the information processing operation (hardware, software, network, etc.). *See also* Application Services.

Client-Server Architecture—Functionality provided by the Distributed Processing Services of CA90s in which applications running on one system request a standard service from another. Client-server relationships differ from application-to-application processing in that there is no peer-level relationship. *See also* Application-to-Application Processing, Cooperative Processing Services and Distributed Processing Services.

Common Communication Interface (CAICCI)—A single, consistent interface that allows communications between Enterprise Software Solutions while insulating the solutions from the specific communications and network protocol requirements within and across the operating systems and hardware platforms. The CA Common Communication Interface supports the various forms of cooperative and distributed information processing. *See also* Distributed Processing Services.

Common Repository Interface (CAICRI)—A full-function interface to CA Repository Services that allows CA software and user programs to populate, navigate and maintain information easily and consistently under the control of the repository. *See also* Repository Services and Integration Services.

Common User Access (CUA)—IBM's standard for user interfacing on designated SAA (Systems Application Architecture) platforms that is endorsed and extended to non-SAA platforms by CA90s. *See also* Systems Application Architecture.

Computer Aided Software Engineering (CASE)—The automation of software development, covering the complete application development life cycle—analysis, design, coding, testing, implementation, maintenance and project management. Front-end CASE tools ("upper CASE") automate the analysis and design processes. Back-end CASE tools ("lower CASE") automate the generation and implementation of code. *See also* Information Management Software.

Computer Associates Graphics Environment (CAGE)—A powerful graphics engine that provides a structure upon which Computer Associates builds and enhances graphics services and standalone graphics solutions with optimum capabilities for each operating system and hardware platform. *See also* Graphics Services.

Computing Architecture For The 90s—*See* CA90s.

Cooperative Processing Services—Functionality provided by the Distributed Processing Services layer of CA90s in which application processing is distributed to different systems. This enables optimal responsiveness, exploitation of the best price/performance technologies for low-volume and high-volume processing, optimal network traffic and realistic security and control. Cooperative Processing Services provide support for application-to-application processing and for client-server architectures. *See also* Application-to-Application Processing, Client-Server Architecture and Distributed Processing Services.

CUA—*See* Common User Access.

Data Center Administration Software—A comprehensive and integrated set of Systems Management Software that enables enterprises to effectively manage enterprise hardware and software inventories and assets and includes the areas of problem/change management, inventory configuration, financial analysis and customization. *See also* Systems Management Software.

Database Management Services—Components of the Integration Services layer of CA90s that provide the functionality of both CA and third-party database management systems to CA Enterprise Software Solutions. *See also* Integration Services.

Database Management Systems—Components of CA Information Management Software that enable both CA and client-written applications to flexibly store, view and manipulate enterprise information. CA Database Management Systems integrate the high production processing capabilities of navigational technology with the flexible ad hoc query facilities of relational technology in a single database management system. *See also* Information Management Software, Relational Technology and Navigational Technology.

Database Server Services—Functionality provided by the Distributed Processing Services layer of CA90s that allows remote access and centralized database management of a multi-user database. *See also* Distributed Processing Services.

Decision Support Tools—Components of the Application Services that support multi-platform financial planning, modeling, reporting and spreadsheet functions. *See also* Application Services.

Dictionary/Repository Support—A centralized facility for consistent and descriptive definitions of corporate information resources. It enables the storing, maintaining and cross-referencing of data as well as impact analysis. Dictionary technology forms the basis of CA Repository Services. *See also* Repository Services and Information Management Software.

Distributed Database Services—Functionality provided by the Distributed Processing Services layer of CA90s, that allows software solutions to access information without regard for the physical location of the data. The database could be local, remote or distributed across several systems. *See also* Distributed Processing Services.

Distributed Information Services—Functionality provided by the Distributed Processing Services layer of CA90s, in which information is made available across multiple operating system platforms. This enables local control and responsiveness combined with global access and centralized control. Distributed Information Services provide support for database server and distributed database. *See also* Distributed Processing Services, Database Server Services and Distributed Database Services.

Distributed Processing Services—The service layer of CA90s that insulates Enterprise Software Solutions from network and protocol requirements and that supports the many forms of distributed processing capabilities. *See also* Cooperative Processing Services, Database Server Services, Distributed Database Services and Common Communication Interface.

Distribution Management Software—The integrated components of CA Business Applications Software that cover a full range of online distribution capabilities for effective control of logistics and warehouse operations, including forecasting and distribution requirements planning. *See also* Business Applications Software.

Enterprise—An organization of any kind, including businesses, government, non-profit organizations, scientific research facilities, academic communities and others that require or can benefit from the utilization of information systems.

Enterprise Software Solutions—The layer of CA90s that comprises an extensive array of integrated software applications that address virtually every aspect of functionality in enterprises and which utilize the Service Layers of CA90s to enhance integration, portability and ease of use. *See also* CA90s, Systems Management Software, Information Management Software and Business Applications Software.

Event Notification Facility (CAIENF)—A component of the Integration Services layer of CA90s that provides "event-" or object-oriented access to operating system and product activity within and across different environments. The Event Notification Facility also provides for the insulation of a software application from the specific operating system on which it executes. Through the sharing of information and the ability of the applications to communicate about activity, the Event Notification Facility enables a higher degree of integration and the automation of functions that previously required manual intervention. *See also* Integration Services.

Expert Systems—A component of the Application Services that provide Enterprise Software Solutions with the ability to automate decision-making. *See also* Application Services.

Financial Management Software—The integrated components of CA Business Applications Software that address the various financial needs of enterprises, including general ledger, accounts receivable, accounts payable, purchasing, inventory control, order processing, fixed assets and financial consolidation, financial modeling, job costing, and labor distribution, as well as fund/encumbrance accounting. *See also* Business Applications Software.

Graphical User Interface (GUI)—Screen presentation that utilizes modern user interfacing techniques commonly found in graphics and desktop applications, and through CA90s User Interface and Visualization Services, is available to Enterprise Software Solutions across mainframe, midrange and desktop systems. Graphical user interfaces utilize such techniques as icons, pop-up menus, dialog boxes, etc. to provide convenience and productivity advantages to end users. *See also* User Interface and Visualization Services.

Graphics Services—Components of the User Interface and Visualization Services layer of CA90s that provide powerful, standard graphics capabilities to Enterprise Software Solutions across operating systems and hardware platforms. *See also* User Interface and Visualization Services and Computer Associates Graphics Environment.

Guiding Principles—The underlying tenets of CA90s that govern new product development, technology acquisition and enhancement of Computer Associates software. *See also* CA90s.

GUI—*See* Graphical User Interface.

Human Resource Management Software—The integrated components of CA Business Applications Software that address the areas of personnel management, payroll, applicant tracking and position control functions. *See also* Business Applications Software.

Information Management Software—The category of Enterprise Software Solutions that integrates data management and software engineering techniques, enabling enterprises to easily build modern applications and access enterprise-wide information. CA Information Management Software includes the areas of Database Management Systems, Dictionary/Repository Support and Software Engineering. *See also* Enterprise Software Solutions.

Integration Services—The service layer of CA90s that supports overall integration among solutions, providing new levels of integration and automation capabilities. *See also* Database Management Services, Repository Services, Event Notification Facility, Standard Security Facility and Application Services.

Islands of Technology—Disparate hardware and software technologies that exist in an enterprise but have not been effectively integrated.

Installation and Maintenance Services—Components of the Application Services that provide standard functions, such as dynamic installation routines, and ensure the accurate and effective installation and maintenance of CA software. *See also* Application Services.

Life Cycle Management Software—The category of Software Engineering (a component of CA Information Management Software) that provides automation and integration of the many tasks required to build large and small applications, including planning, controlling and reporting on applications, application components, versions, configurations, resources, tools, people, schedules, etc. *See also* Software Engineering and Information Management Software.

Manufacturing Management Software—The integrated components of CA Business Applications Software that address the needs of manufacturers in discrete and repetitive environments as well as those in the aerospace and defense industries. Areas covered include bill of material, cost control, forecast management, order entry, distribution requirements planning, inventory control, material requirements planning, master production scheduling, shop floor control and purchasing management. *See also* Business Applications Software.

NAS—*See* Network Application Support.

Navigational Technology—Traditional database access methods such as hierarchical, network and inverted list, that offer superior high-volume transaction processing capabilities. Both navigational and relational technologies are available in a single database management system through CA Database Management Systems. *See also* Relational Technology and Database Management Systems.

Network Application Support (NAS)—Digital Equipment Corporation's software architecture that defines standards for applications across Digital platforms.

Online Consultant—A component of User Interface Management Services that, through a PC-based workstation, provides multimedia (including video) tutorials and context-sensitive help and advice during the use of CA Enterprise Software Solutions. *See also* User Interface Management Services.

Open Software Foundation (OSF)—An industry organization with the mission to define reference implementations and specifications for a portable operating environment. Its OSF/1 operating system implementation complies with the POSIX, X/Open and SVID standards; the OSF/Motif user interface standard sits on top of the X Window System. Many major UNIX systems vendors have made commitments to migrate to OSF/1.

Performance Management and Accounting Software—A complete and integrated set of Systems Management Software that addresses performance management, resource accounting and capacity planning for operating systems, networks and subsystems such as CICS and DASD, as well as for database management systems. *See also* Systems Management Software.

Platforms—The variety of operating systems and hardware environments spanning mainframes, midrange and desktop systems on which Enterprise Software Solutions execute. Through the capabilities offered by the Service Layers, CA90s promotes distributed processing and portability of Enterprise Software Solutions across the widest range of platforms. *See also* CA90s, Enterprise Software Solutions and Service Layers.

POSIX—An official standard defining the Application Program Interface (API) for a portable operating system/application environment, defined by IEEE under charter by ANSI. To date only the standard for the *kernel*, or base operating system, API has been adopted; other API standards are in progress. POSIX has a lot in common with SVID.

Product Validation Interface (CAIPVI)—A component of the Application Services that ensures the correct installation and runtime integrity of CA and other vendor-supplied software. *See also* Application Services.

Project Management Tools—A wide range of facilities, available across multiple platforms that provide end users with consistent techniques and methodologies for forecasting, planning, optimizing and controlling resources, costs and schedules related to application development projects. *See also* Application Services.

Relational Technology—Database access techniques that provide extensive data access flexibility through the use of SQL. Both relational and navigational technologies are available in a single database management system through CA Database Management Systems. *See also* Navigational Technology and Database Management Systems.

Reporting Services—Components of the User Interface and Visualization Services layer of CA90s that provide consistent, comprehensive and integrated reporting capabilities for Enterprise Software Solutions across multiple platforms. Reporting Services support sophisticated processing and advanced function printing. *See also* User Interface and Visualization Services and Advanced Function Printing.

Repository Services—A component of the Integration Services layer of CA90s that provides global dictionary facilities for sharing information across all CA Enterprise Software Solutions and across multiple platforms. Repository Services also support other vendor repositories such as IBM's Repository Manager/MVS and Digital's CDD/Repository. *See also* Integration Services.

SAA—*See* Systems Application Architecture.

Security, Control and Audit Software—A comprehensive and integrated set of Systems Management Software that addresses the complete protection of data and resources including access control and auditing capabilities across networks. *See also* Systems Management Software.

Service and Support Facilities—Components of the Application Services that provide extensive online service, support and training facilities for client data centers. *See also* Application Services.

Service Layers—Key components of CA90s that provide shared functions and technologies for integrated Enterprise Software Solutions and that enable the software to operate across the widest range of platforms. *See also* User Interface and Visualization Services, Integration Services and Distributed Processing Services.

Single-Point Signon—A facility that enables users to identify themselves at one point in a network, without requiring additional signons when accessing individual applications, no matter where those applications reside. Internal signons are handled transparently by propagating user IDs and passwords as needed. *See also* Application Services.

Single-Point User Registration—A facility that speeds up and simplifies the task of registering users with appropriate applications by providing a single point of registration across multiple operating systems. *See also* Application Services.

Software Architecture—*See* Architecture.

Software Engineering—A category of Information Management Software that addresses the full range of software development activities, including Life Cycle Management Software and Application Development Systems. *See also* Information Management Software, Life Cycle Management Software and Application Development Systems.

SQL—Structured Query Language. A database definition and manipulation language that offers easier end-user access to enterprise data stored in database management systems using relational technology.

SQL Interface (CAISQI)—An application programming interface (API) to CA and third-party SQL databases supporting CA Extended SQL and other SQL implementations. *See also* CA Extended SQL and Relational Technology.

Standard Security Facility (CAISSF)—A component of the Integration Services layer of CA90s that provides Enterprise Software Solutions with a single external security mechanism for controlling and monitoring access to all system and application resources and processes. The CA Standard Security Facility utilizes the extensive services of the industry-leading security products, CA-ACF2 and CA TOP-SECRET, and can be used in addition to or in place of product-specific controls. *See also* Integration Services.

SVID—The "System V Interface Definition" from AT&T defines the API for their version of UNIX.

Systems Application Architecture (SAA)—The IBM initiative that describes standards for software development with the purpose of enabling software to be portable across specified IBM operating system and hardware platforms.

Systems Management Software—The category of Enterprise Software Solutions that provide functionality for automating all critical areas of the data center. CA Systems Management Software includes the areas of Automated Production Control; Automated Storage Management; Performance Management and Accounting; Data Center Administration; and Security, Control and Audit. *See also* Enterprise Software Solutions.

UNIX International—An organization of companies focusing on AT&T's System V as the reference implementation for the UNIX operating system.

User Interface and Visualization Services—The service layer of CA90s that provides functionality to ensure a consistent look and feel of software solutions and that insulates end users from the complexities of underlying technologies. *See also* User Interface Management Services, Graphics Services, Reporting Services and Voice Services.

User Interface Management Services (CAIUIMS)—Components of the User Interface and Visualization Services layer of CA90s that provide a consistent look and feel for all Enterprise Software Solutions and that support modern user interfacing techniques. *See also* User Interface and Visualization Services.

Voice Services—Components of the User Interface and Visualization Services layer of CA90s that utilize advanced technologies to provide voice-based systems that can be utilized by Enterprise Software Solutions as user-interfacing tools. *See also* User Interface and Visualization Services.

X/Open—An industry organization made up of virtually all corporations involved in UNIX with the mission to define a de facto standard for an operating system API, the *Common Applications Environment* (CAE). Its foundation is POSIX, but X/Open extends the scope of POSIX to include data management, application integration, data communications, distributed processing, high-level languages and the X Window System.

X Window System—From MIT, defines the technical services for a graphical user interfacing system. X is portable and supports distributed processing. It does not define the "look and feel" or high-level end-user functions, which are provided by OSF/Motif and Open Look.